Roughly thirty miles west of the Golden Gate Bridge lay the Farallon Islands, or Farallones in Spanish meaning pillars or sea cliffs. Known as the 'Islands of the Dead' by the natives of the area, this small group of rocky islets can be seen on clear days by San Francisco residents and visitors, especially by those driving the Great Highway or looking out their highest windows in the Western Addition of The City. Many of the collection of tiny islands sport natural bridges of relatively small sizes and, while not popularly known for this, will seem to sing to those on land when the wind and humidity are just right. Thus, Homer's Odyssey comes to mind and its daughters of the river god Achelos named Terpsichore, Melpomene, Sterope, and Chthon. These sirens are known to often create enchanting music and voices to lure sailors passing by to shipwreck on their islands.

The Sirens
Of
Farallon Islands

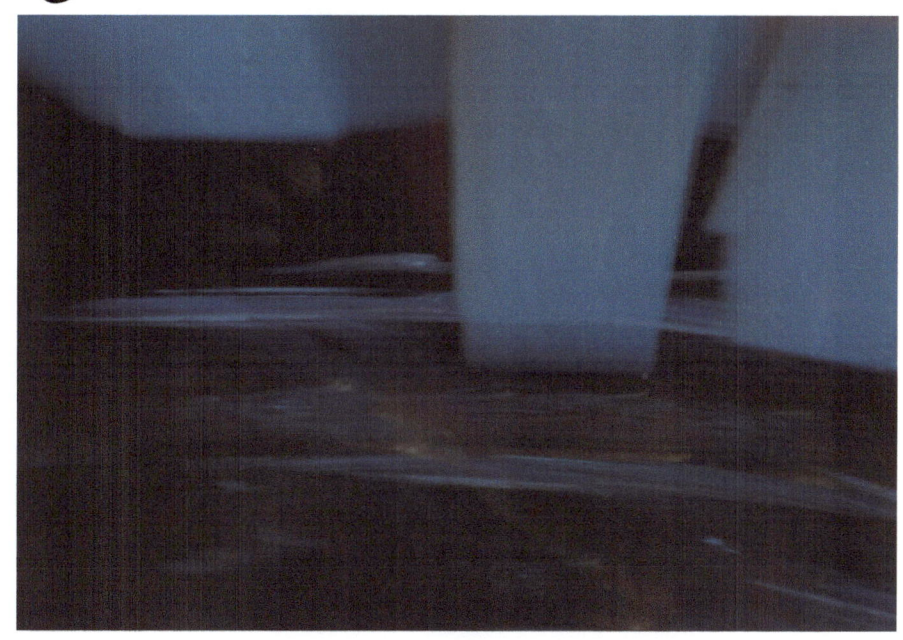

Photographs
By
David Cope

The Sirens of Farallon Islands
Photographs by David Cope

Epoc Books
Printed in the United States of America
© David Cope 2016
Published 2016.

This book is dedicated to my wife, sons, and grandchildren, Zoe, Tess, Gavin, and Ethan whose excitement for everyday things never ceases to amaze me. And to those older kids like me who believe in those children.

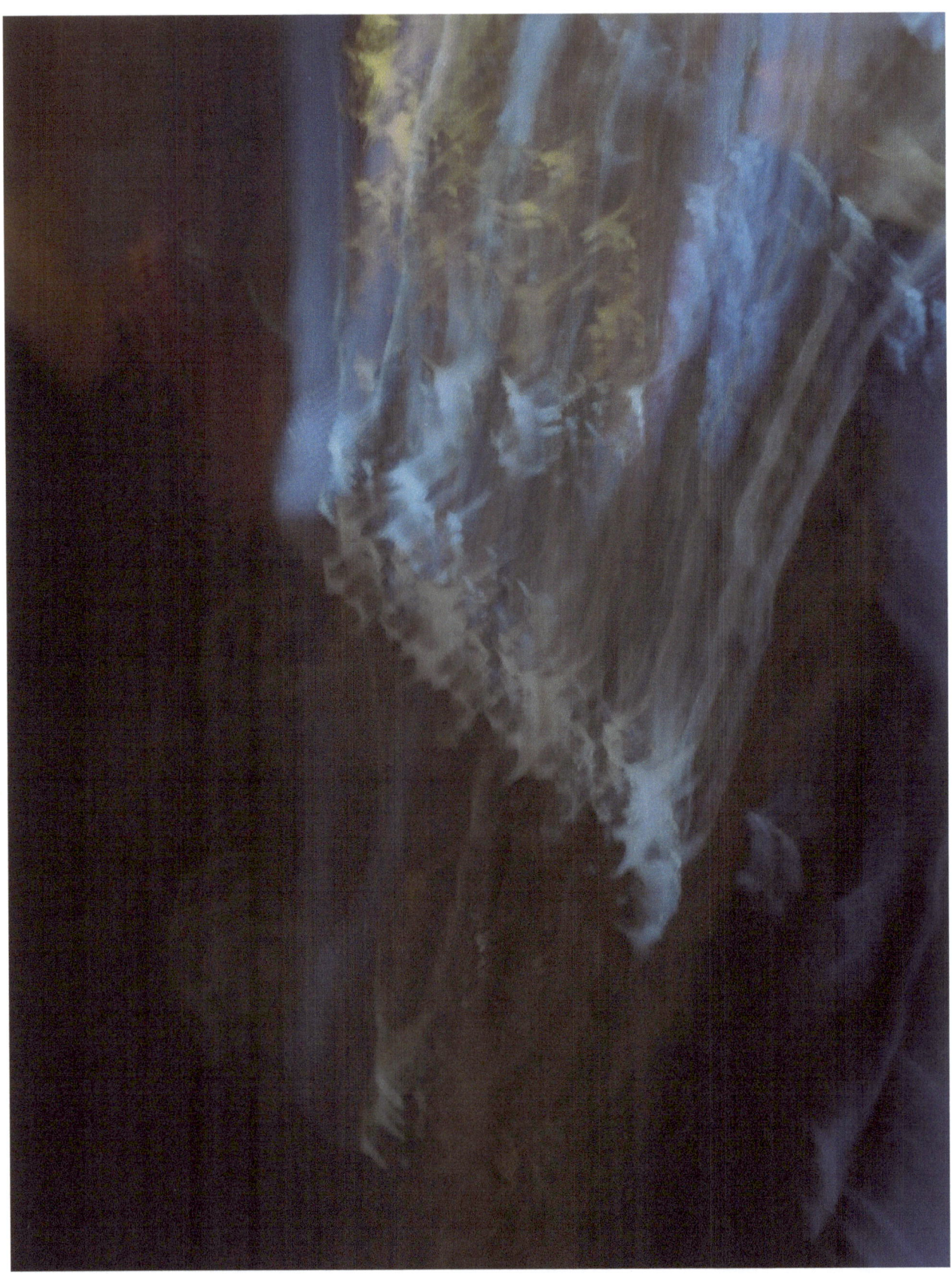

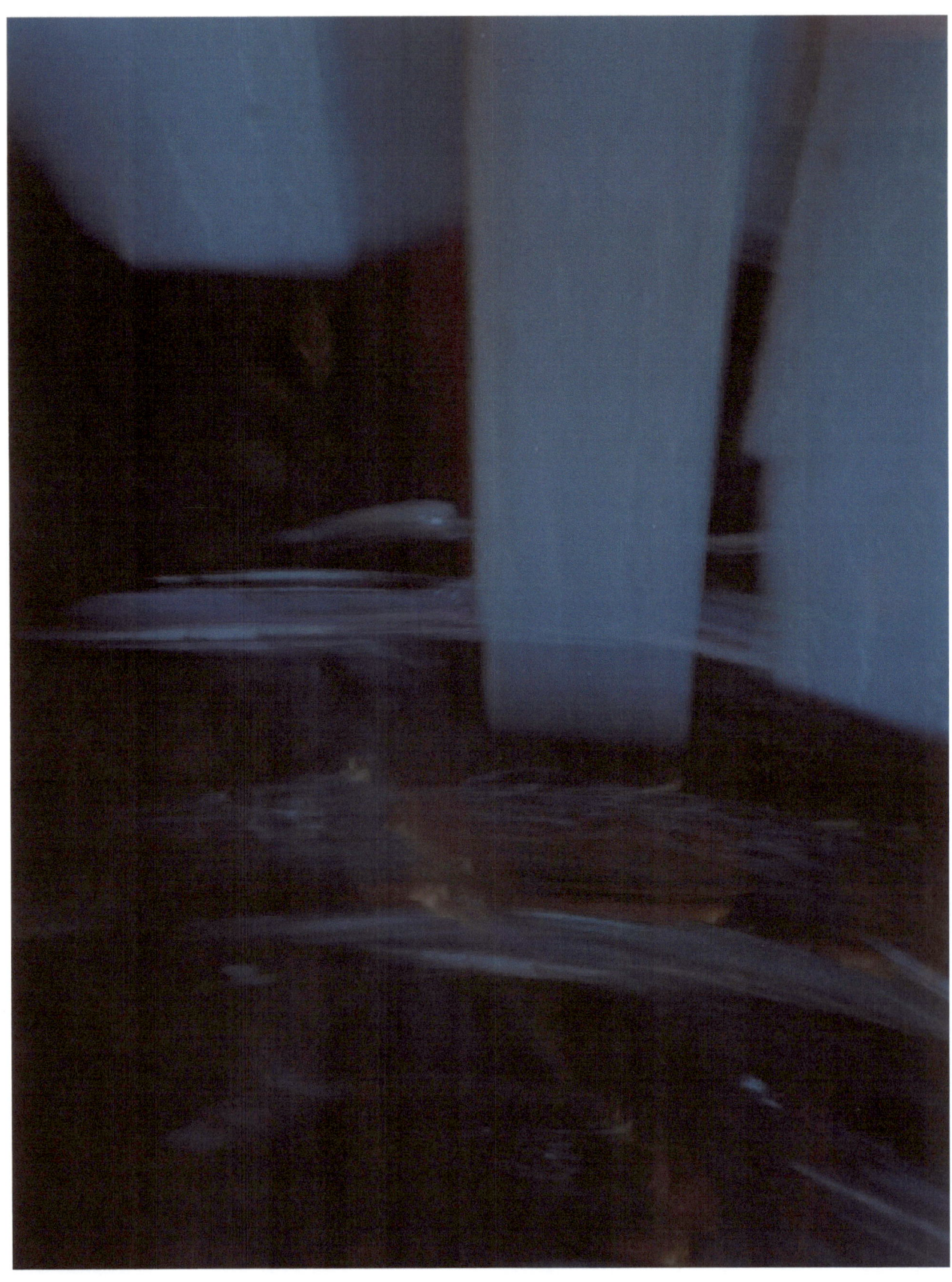

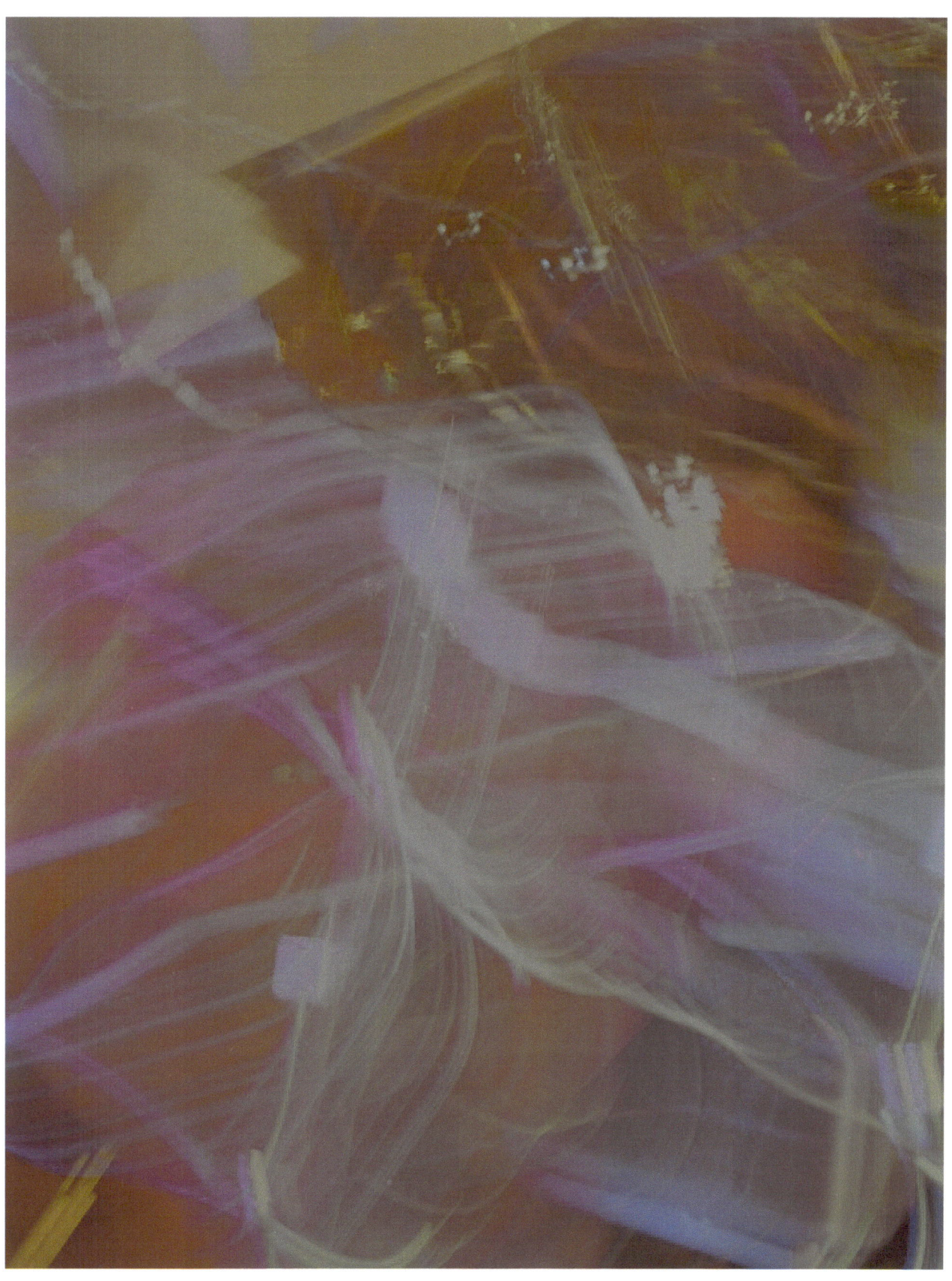

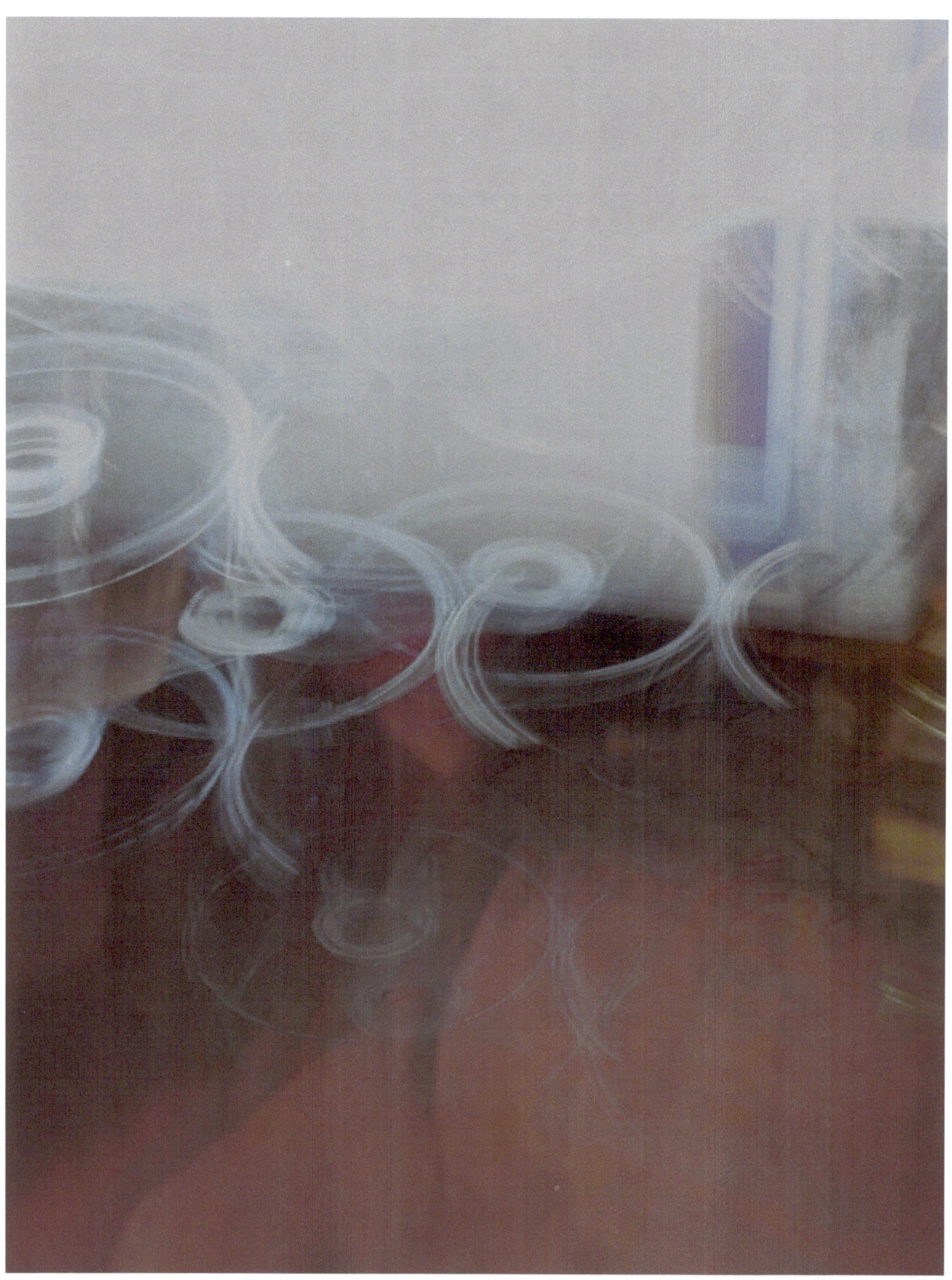

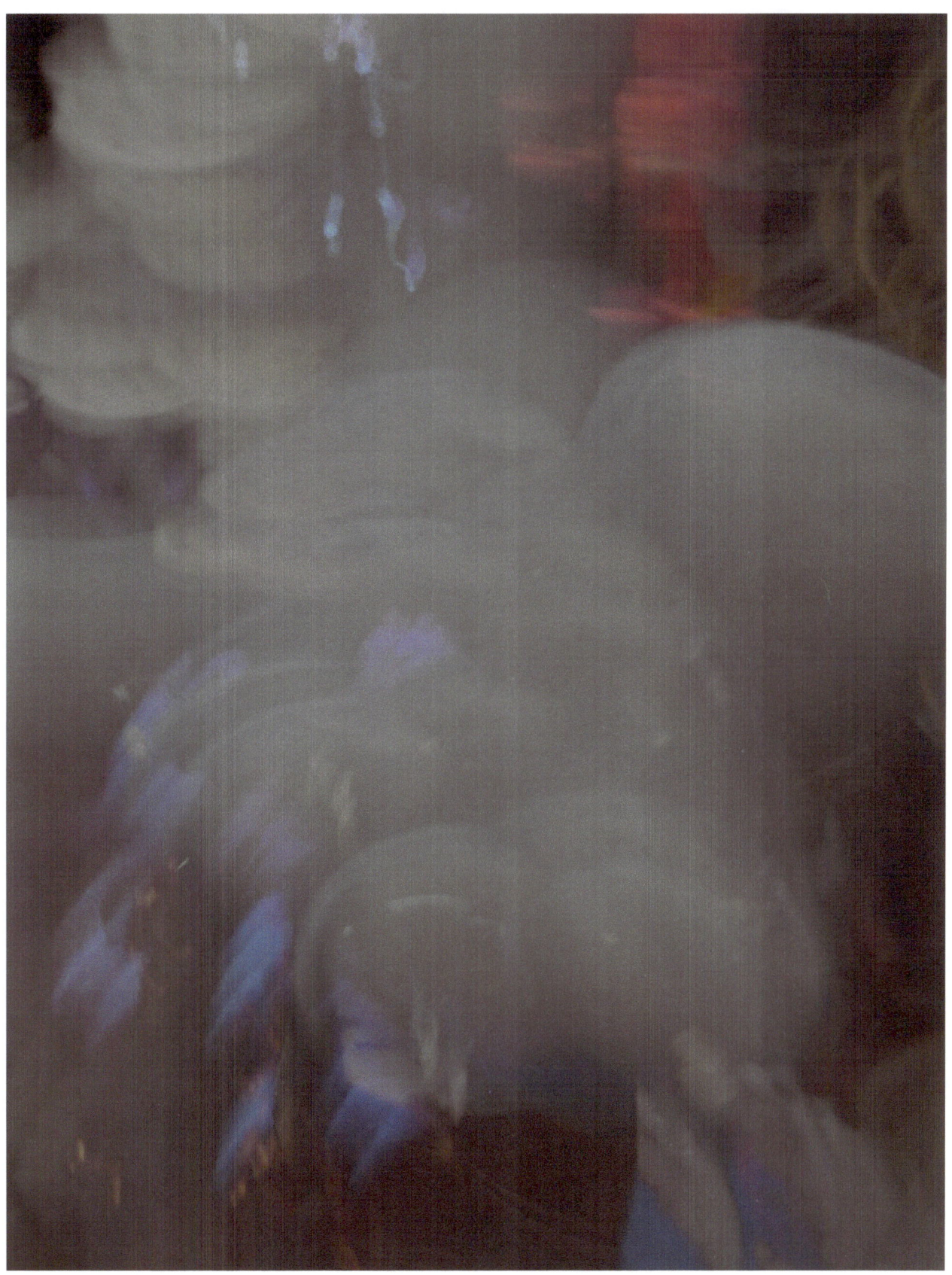

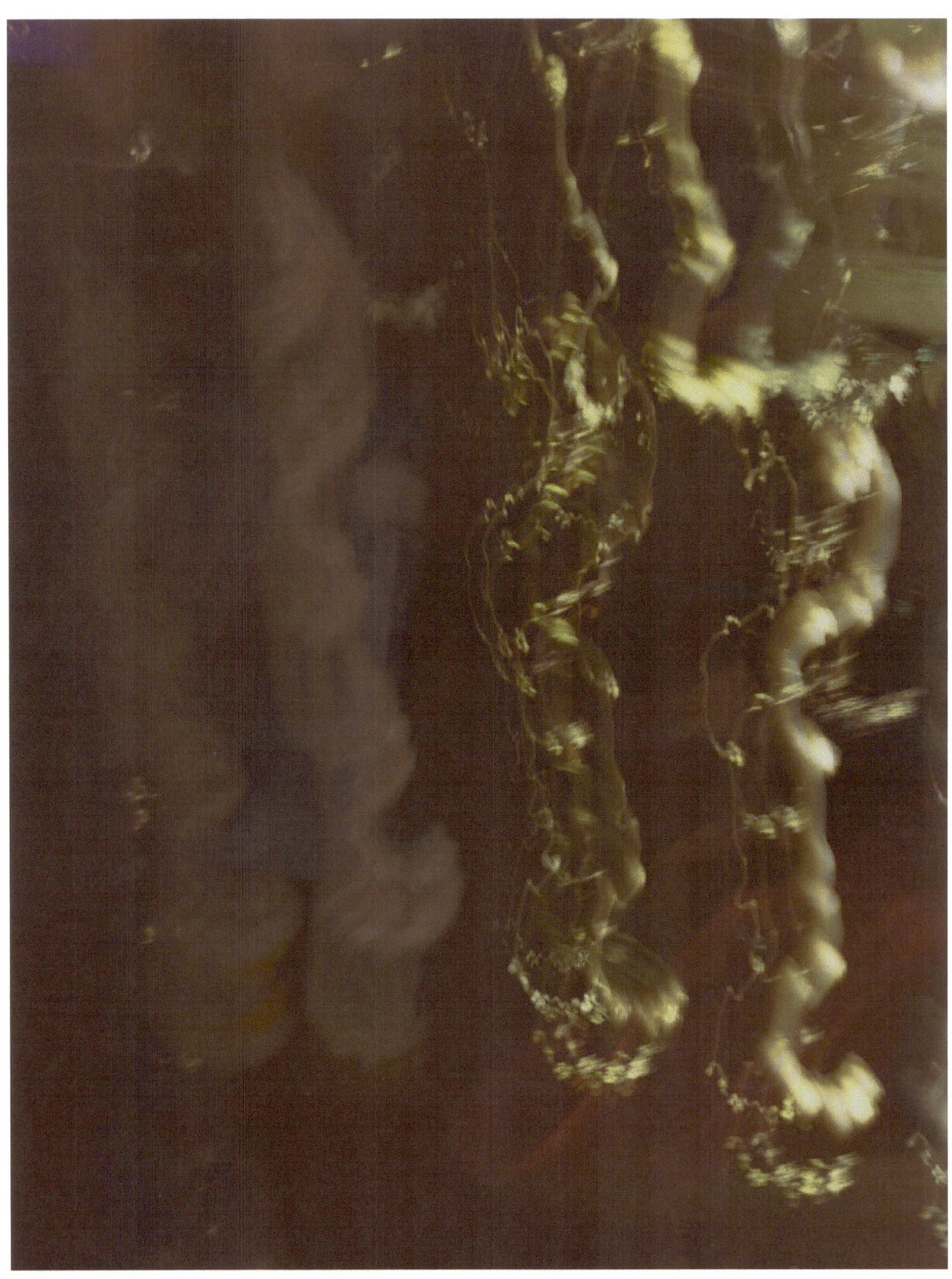

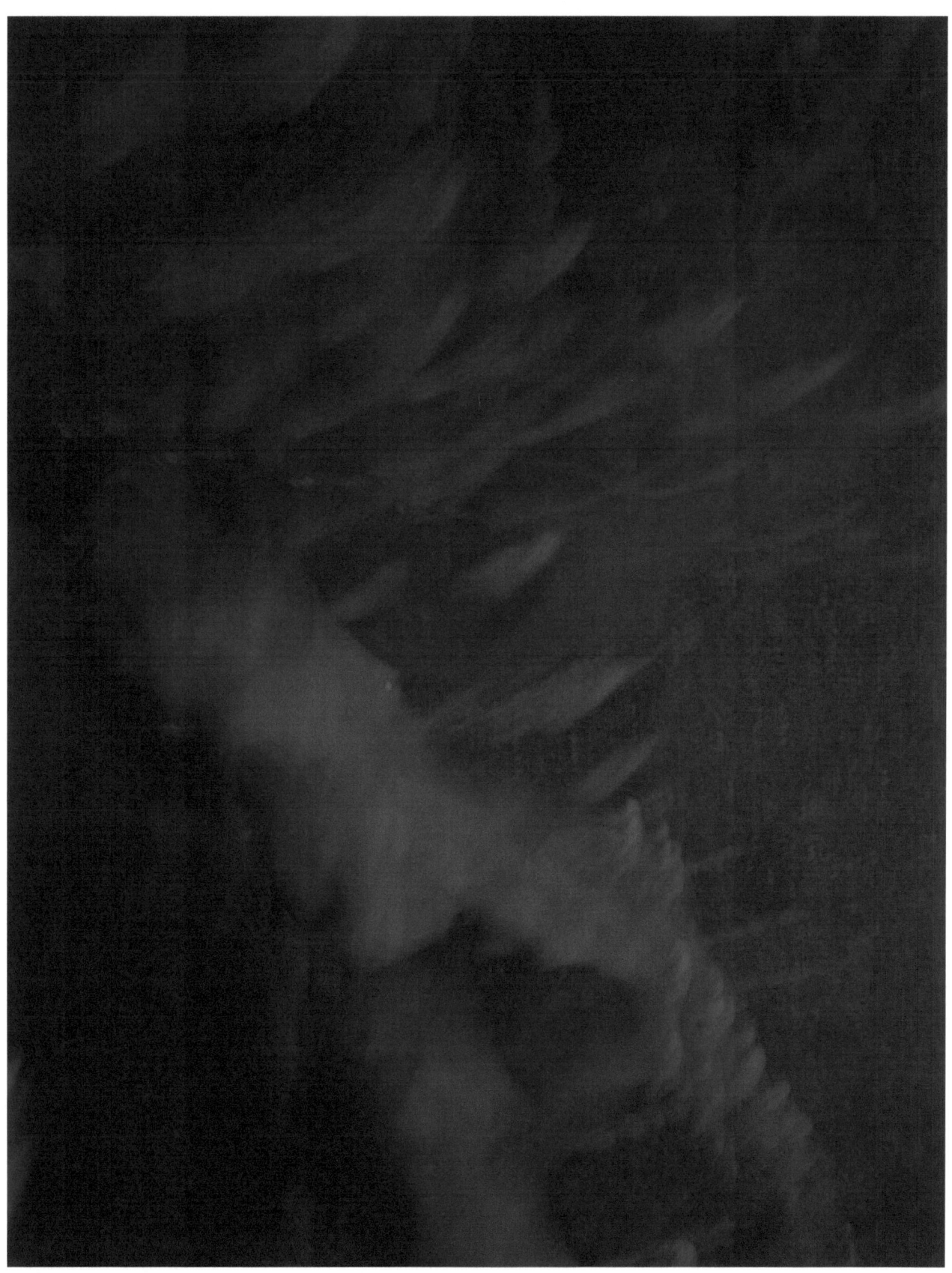

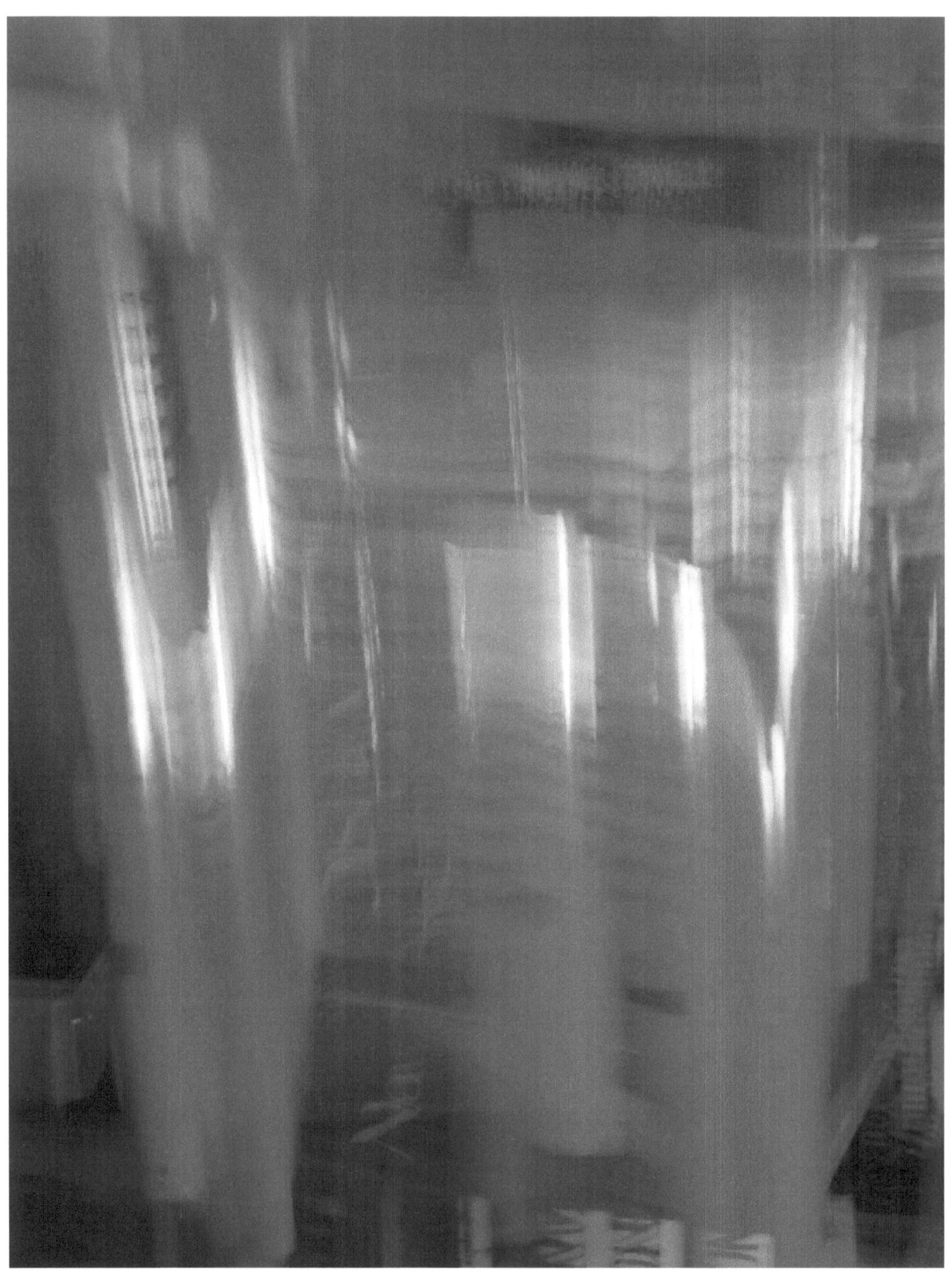

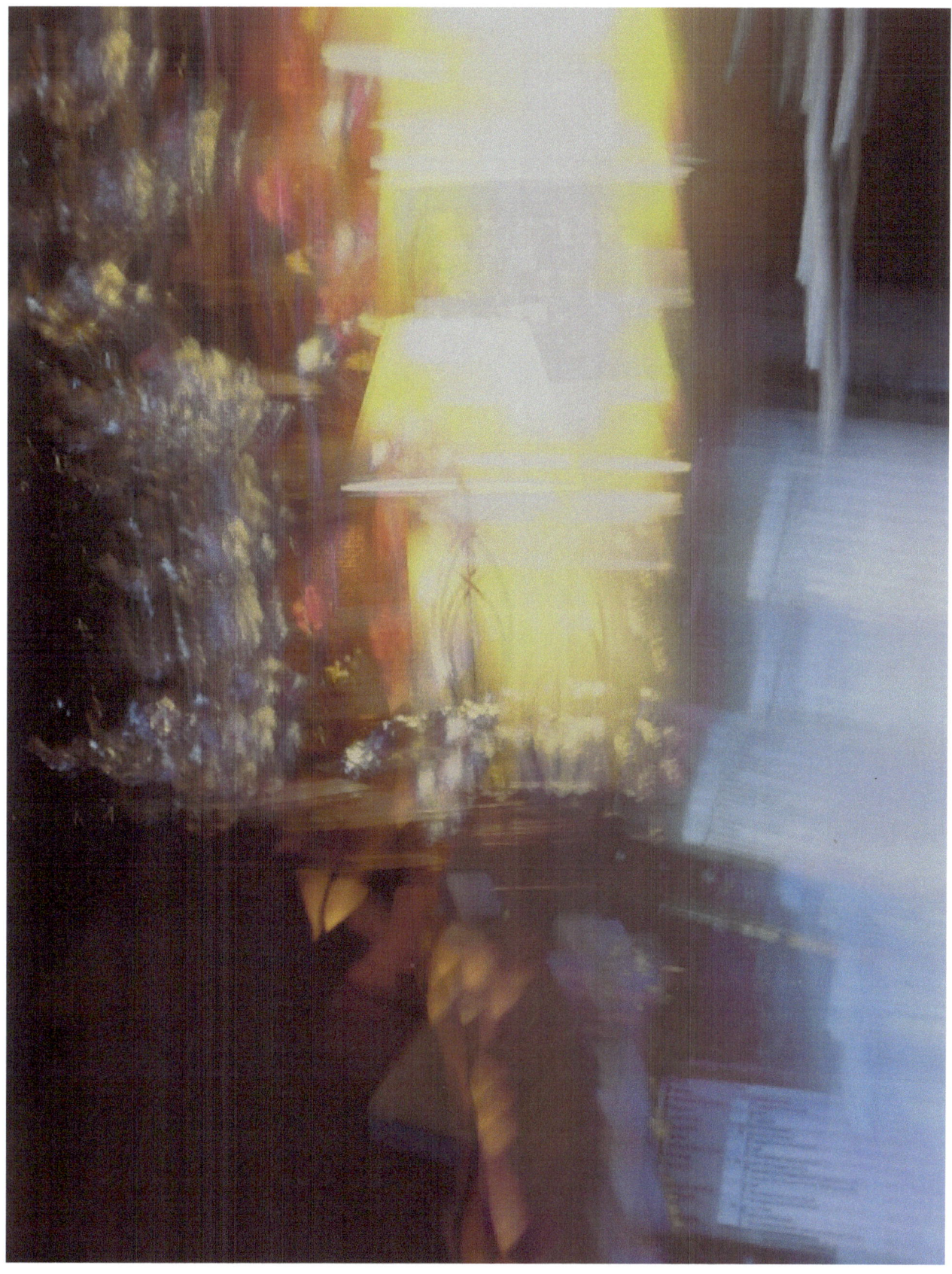

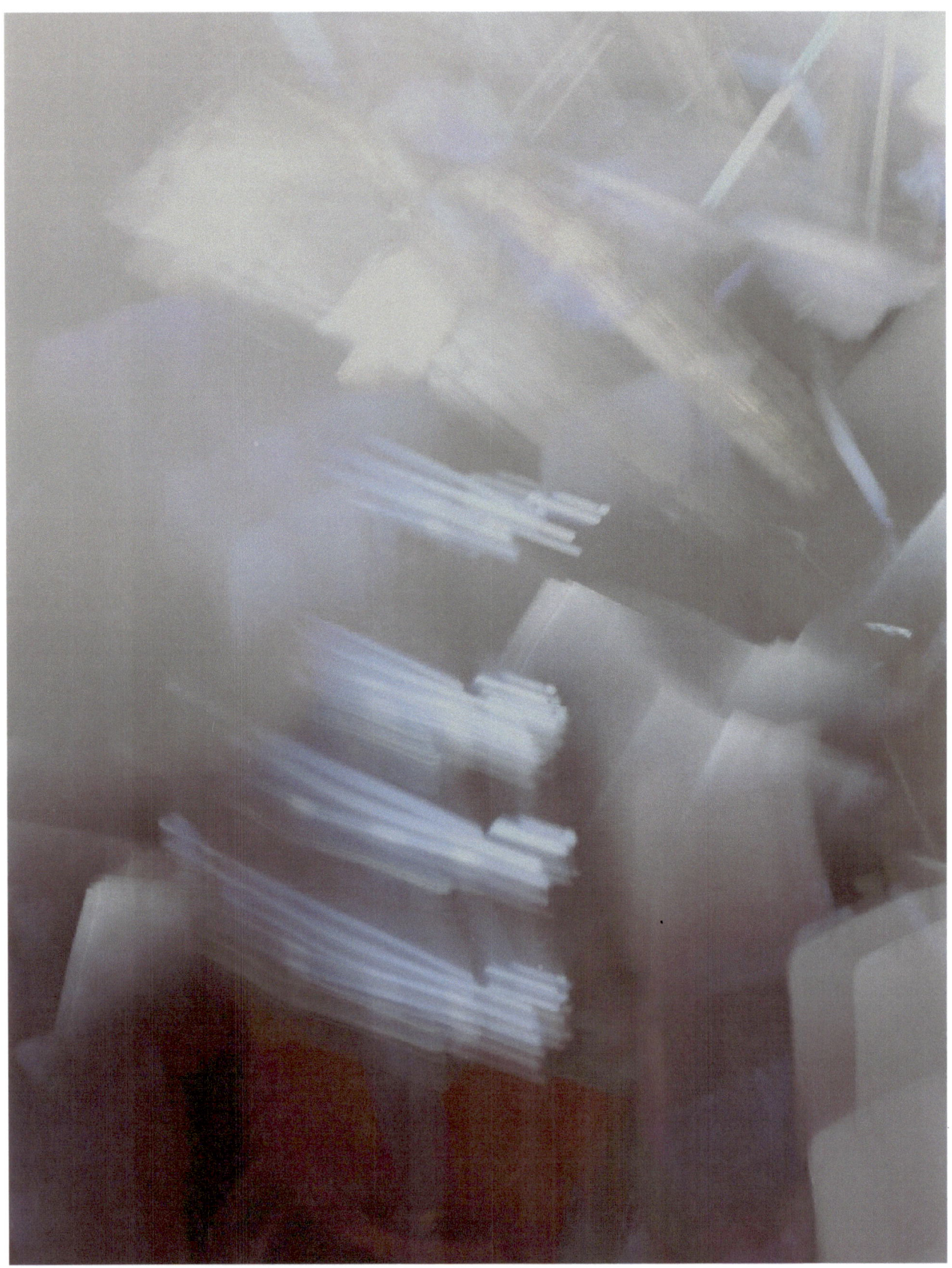

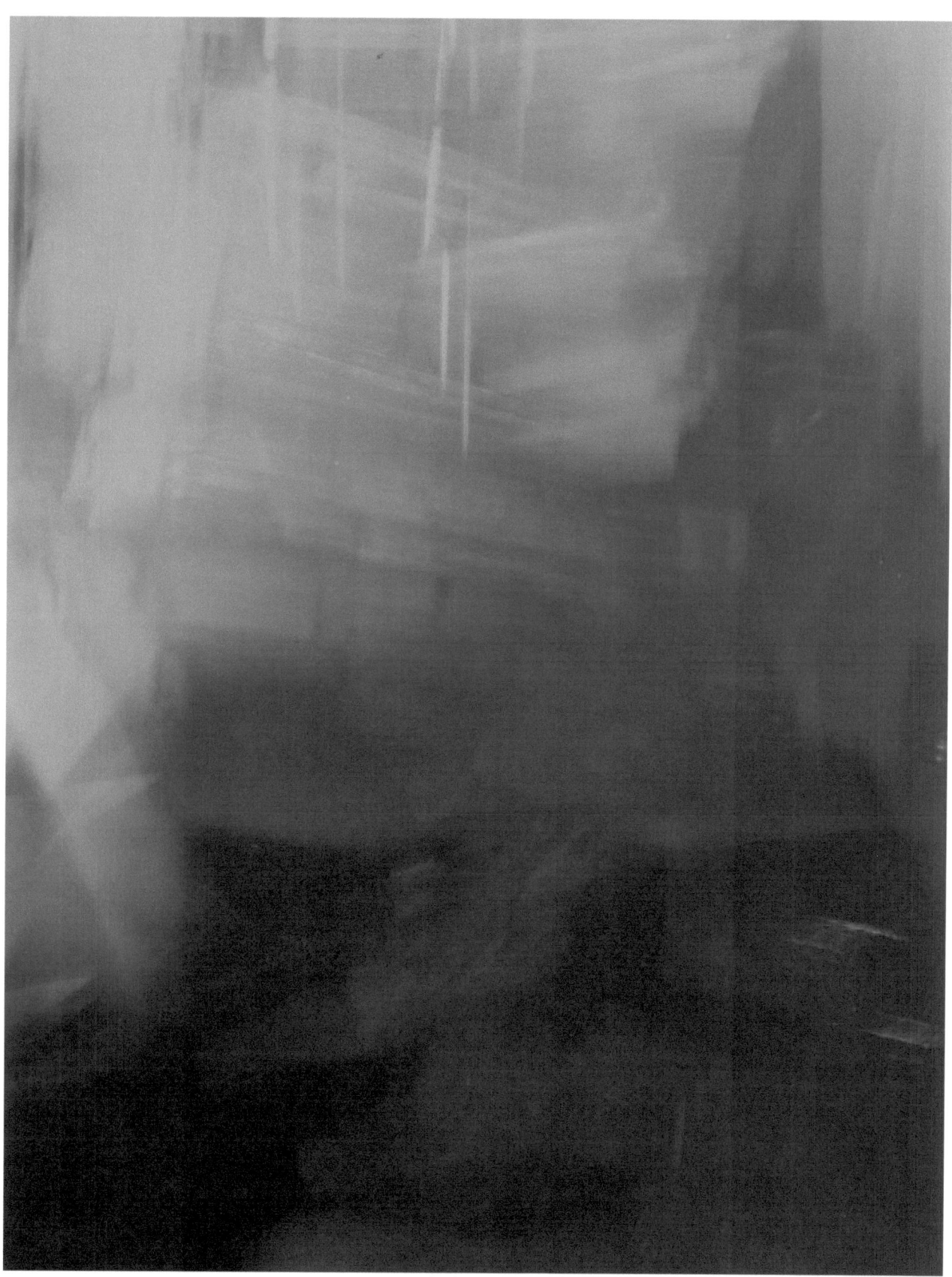

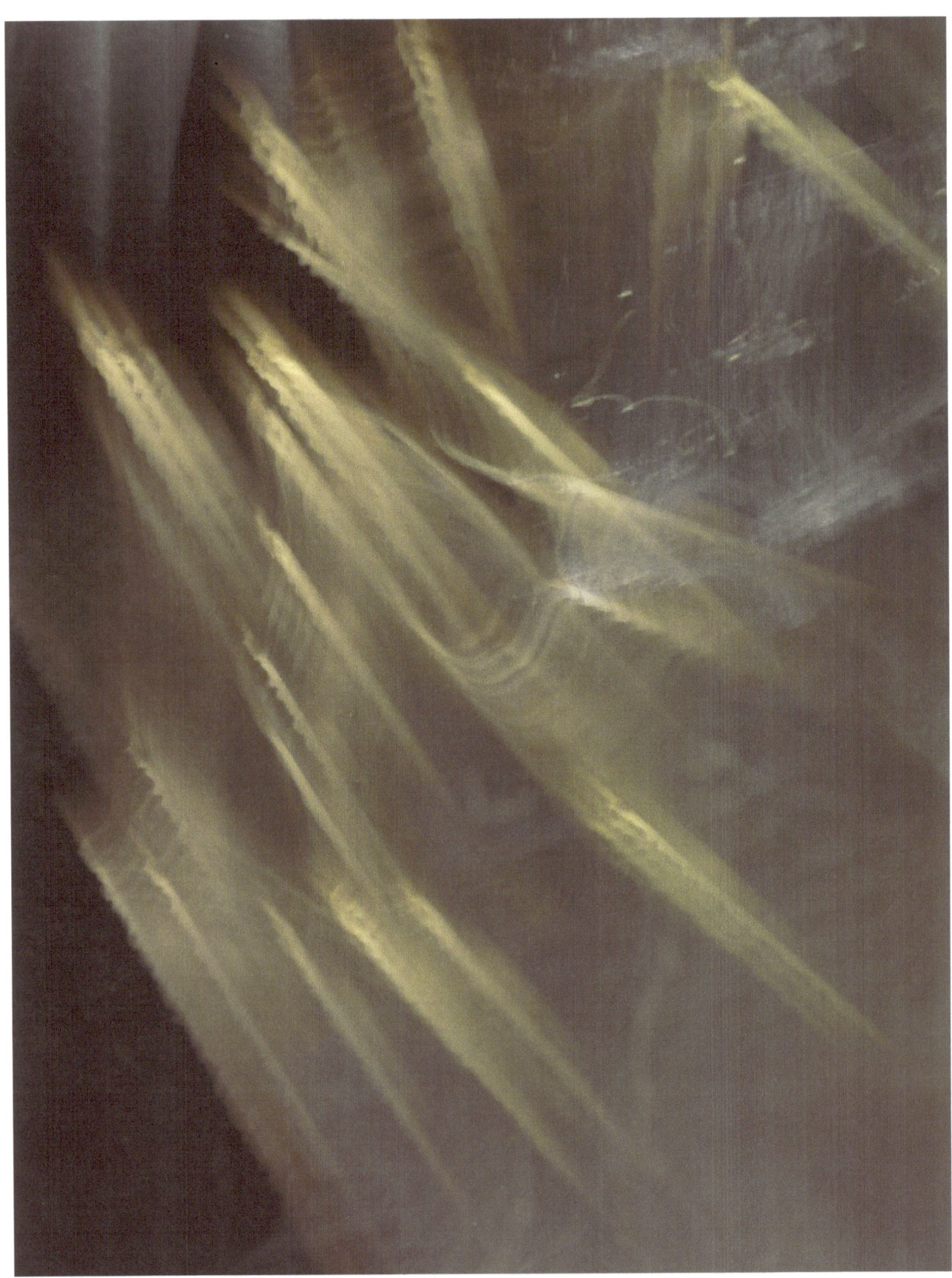

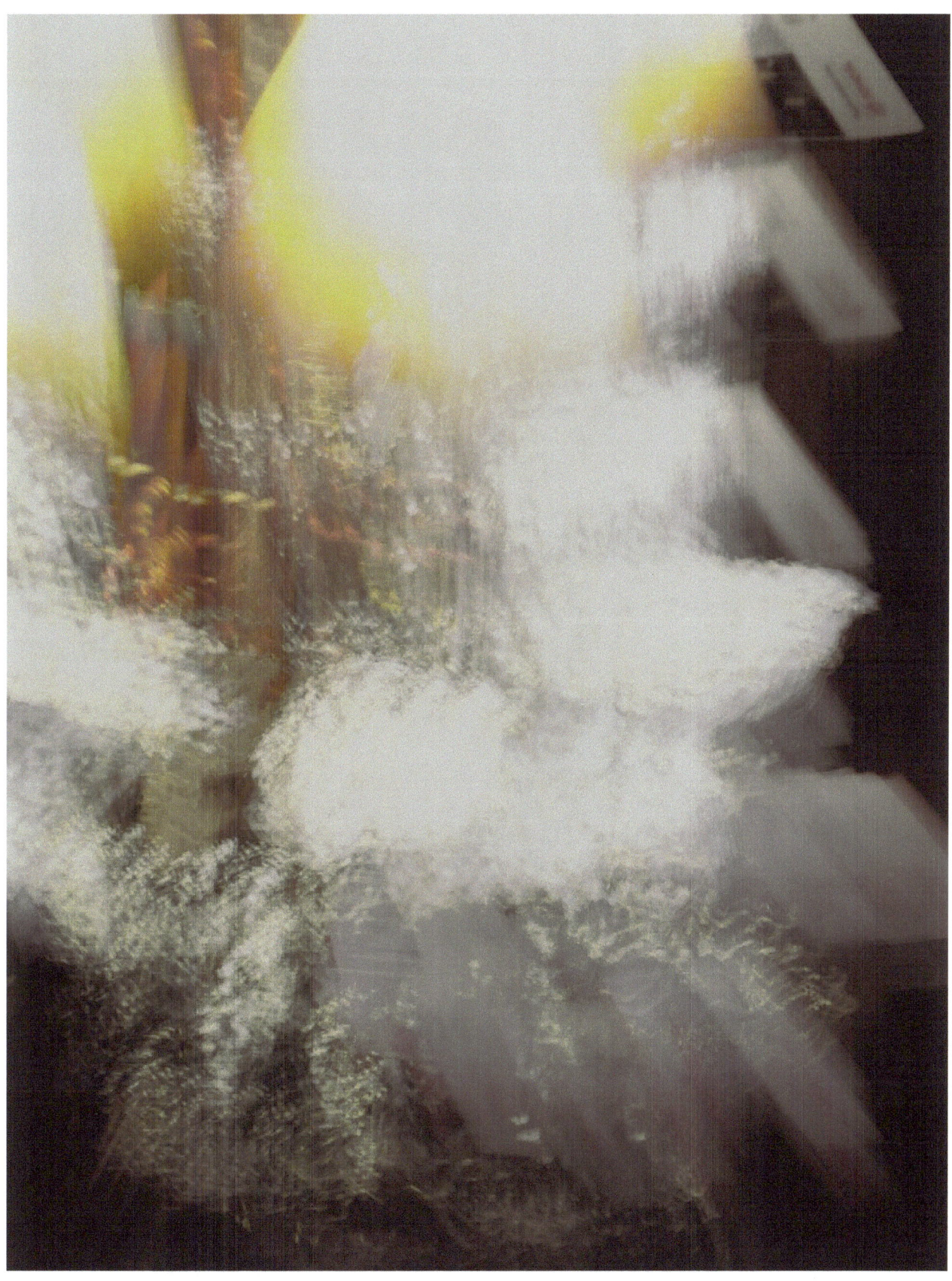

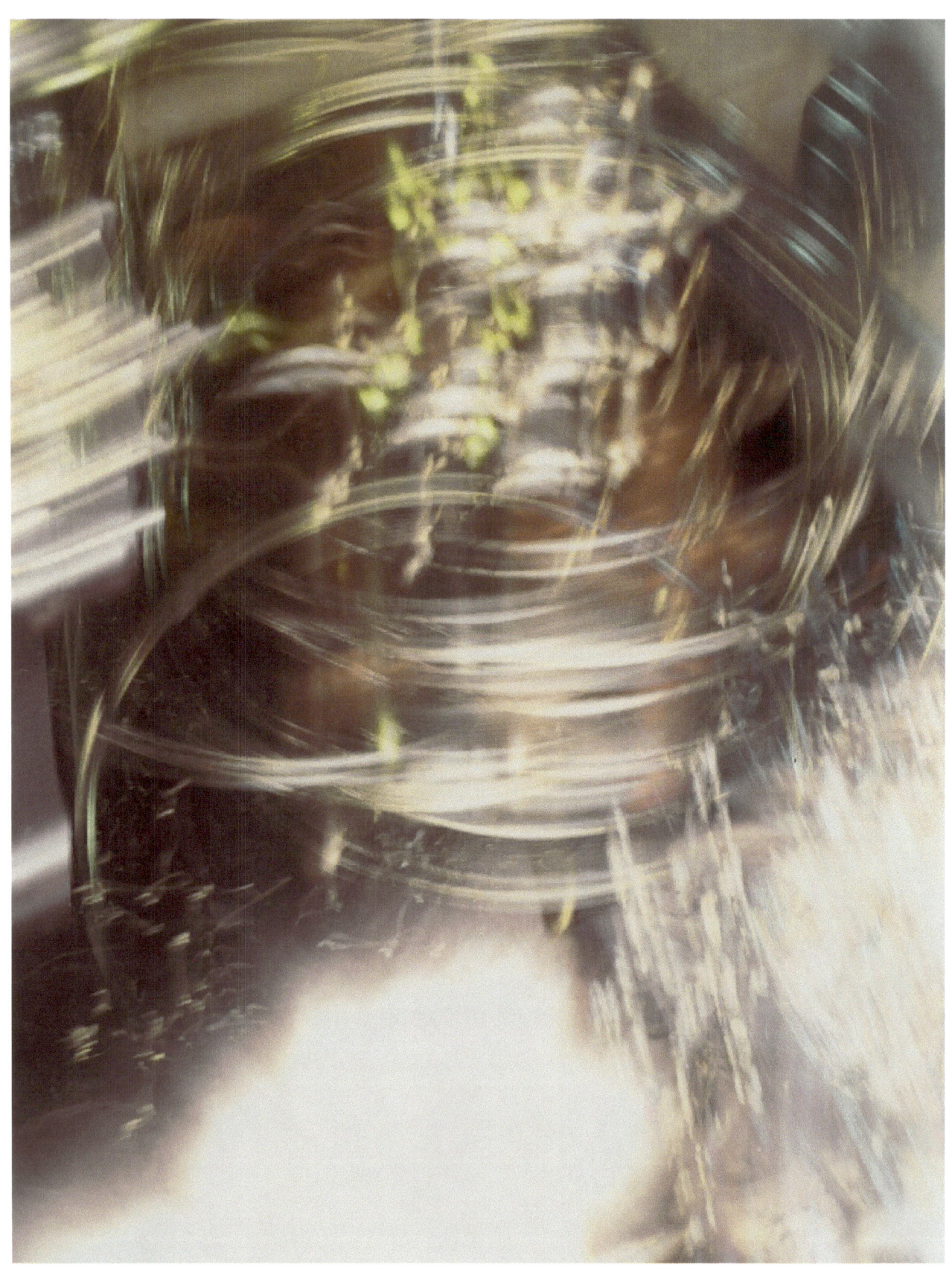

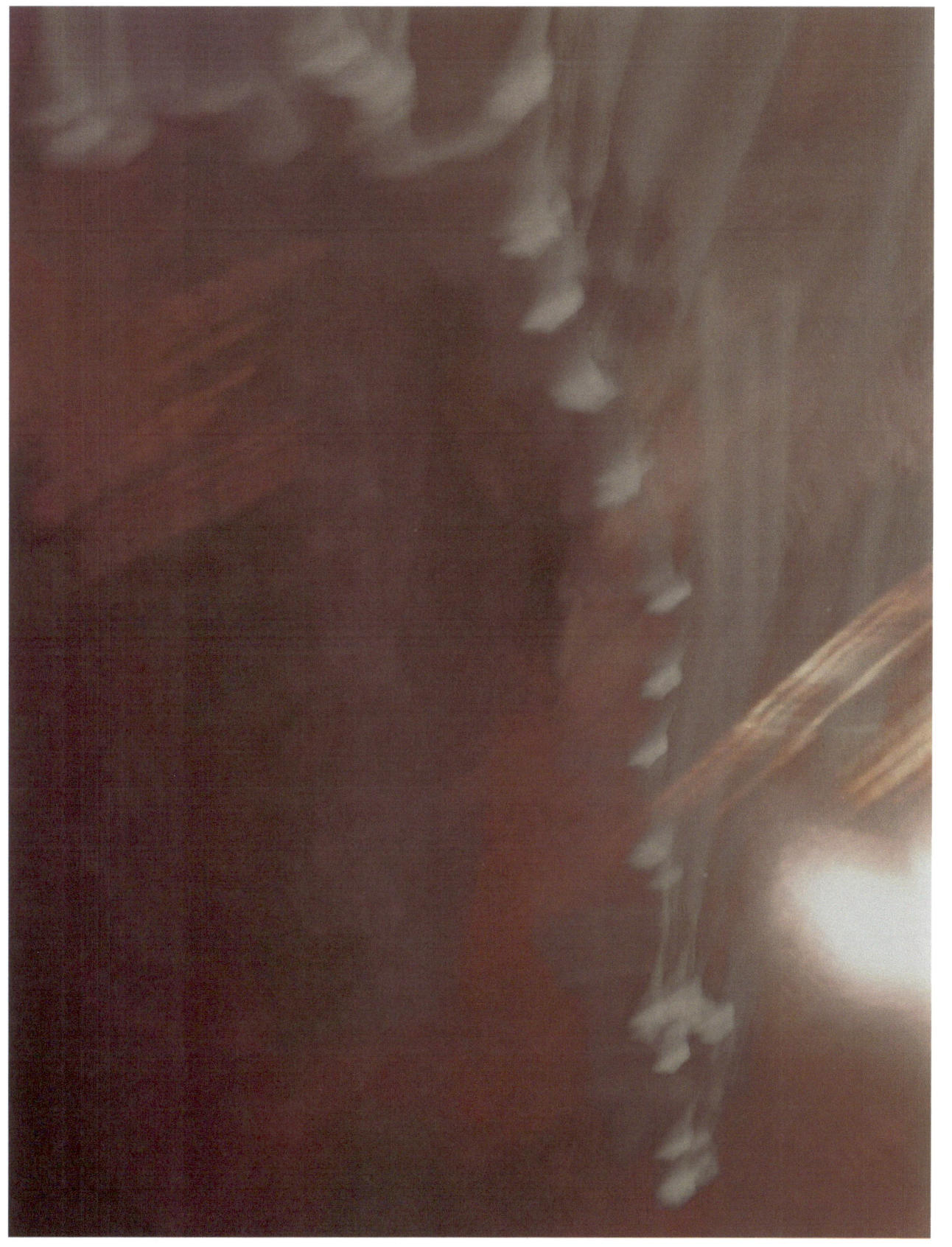

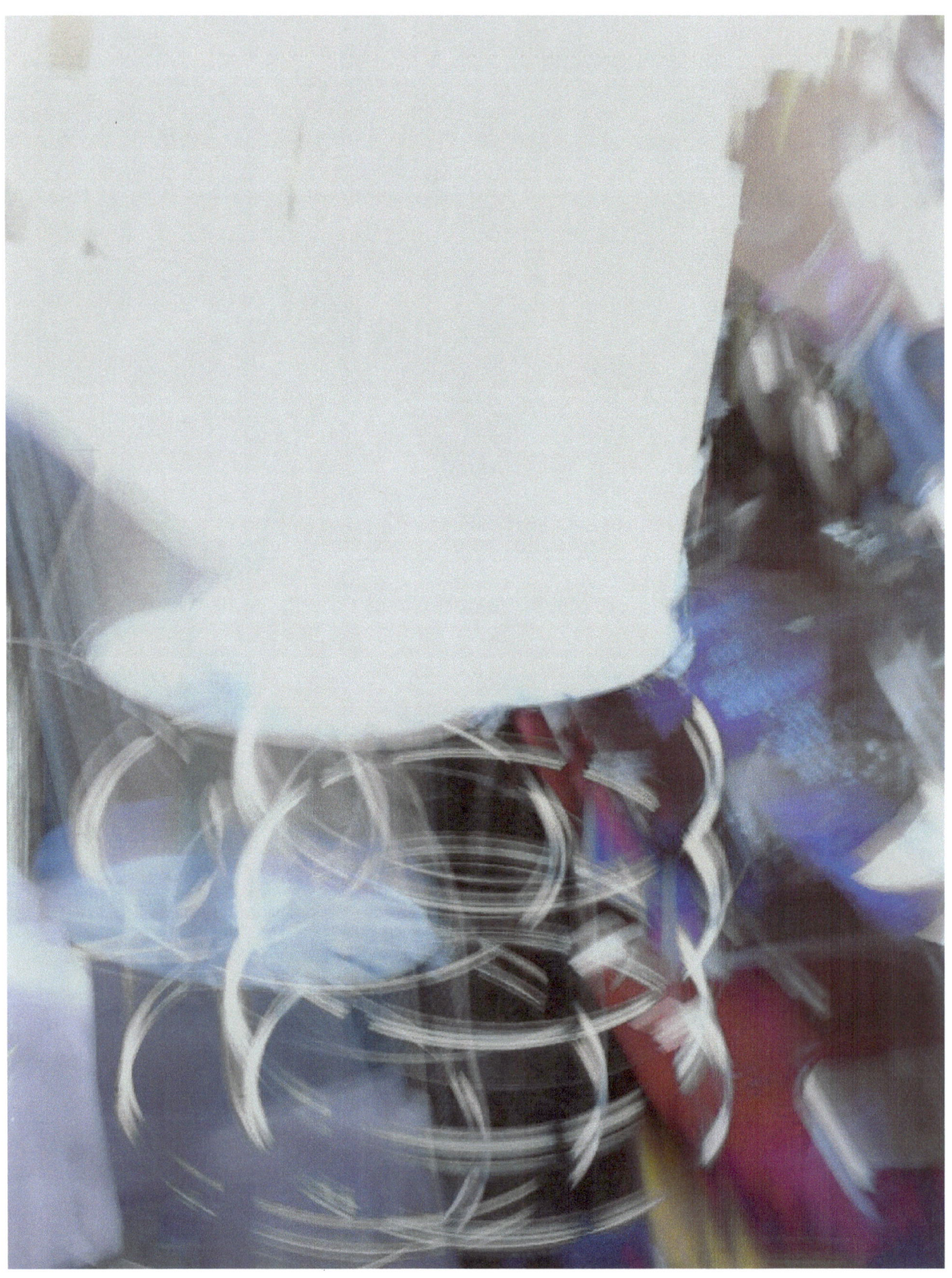

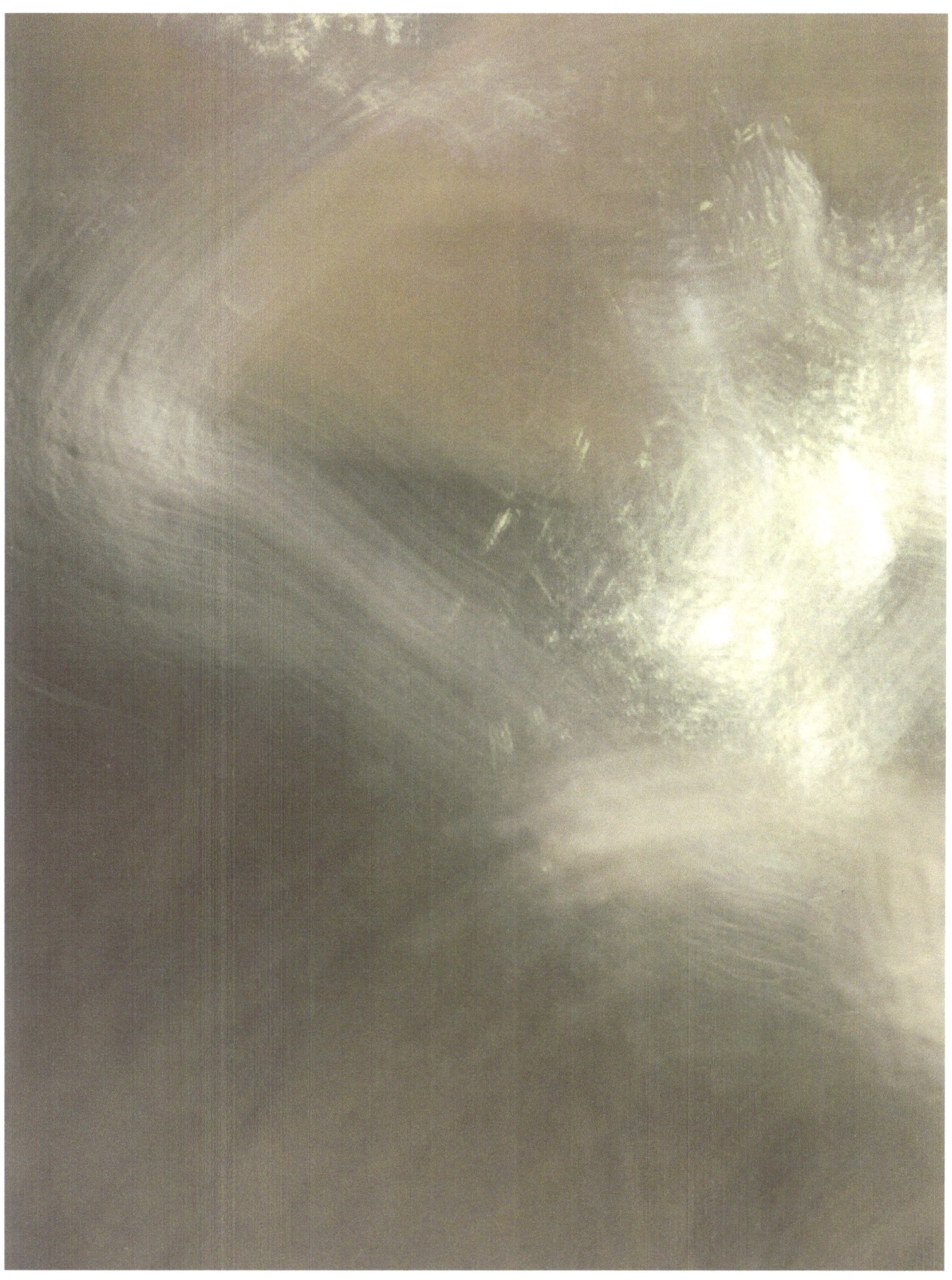

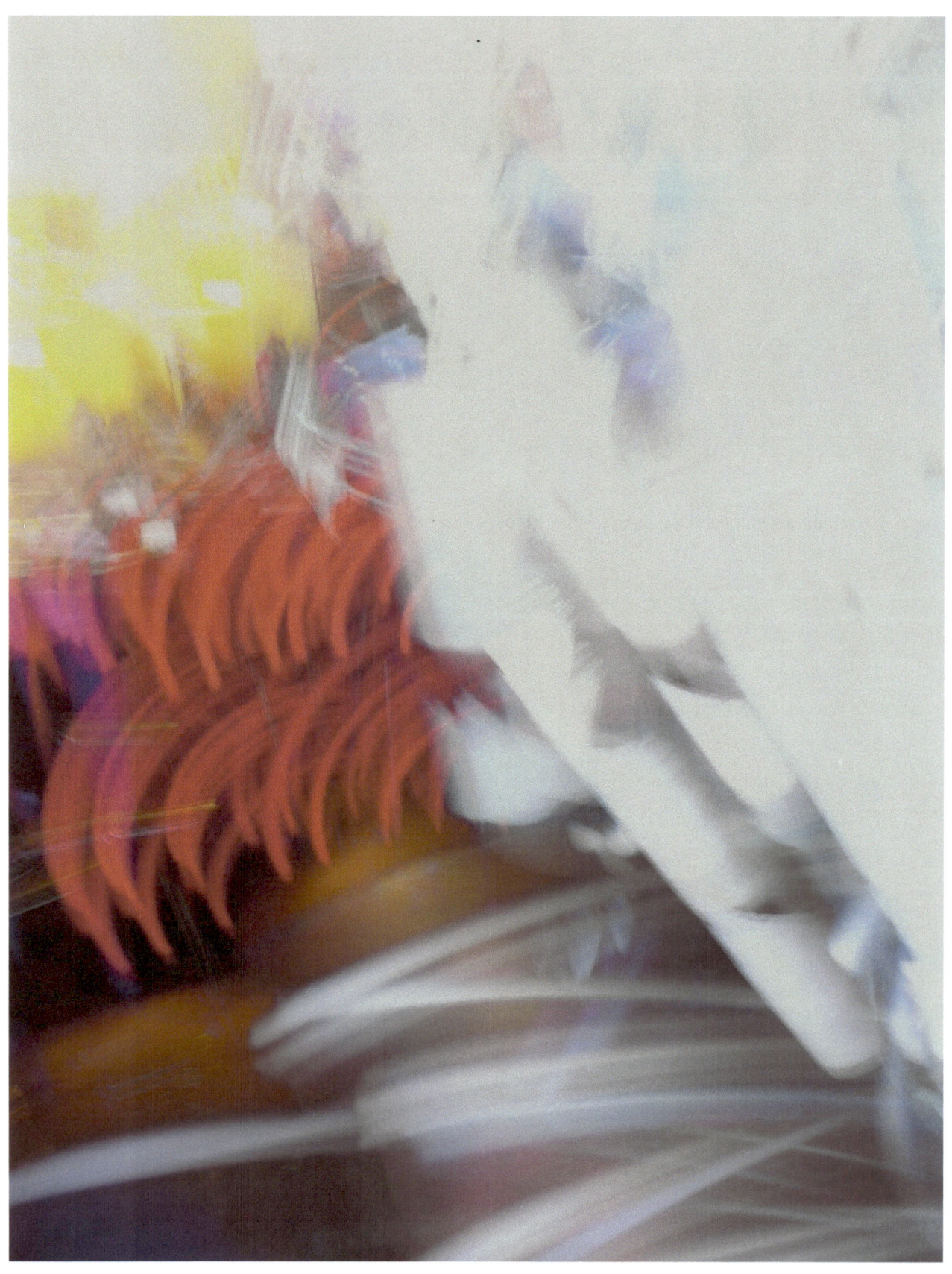

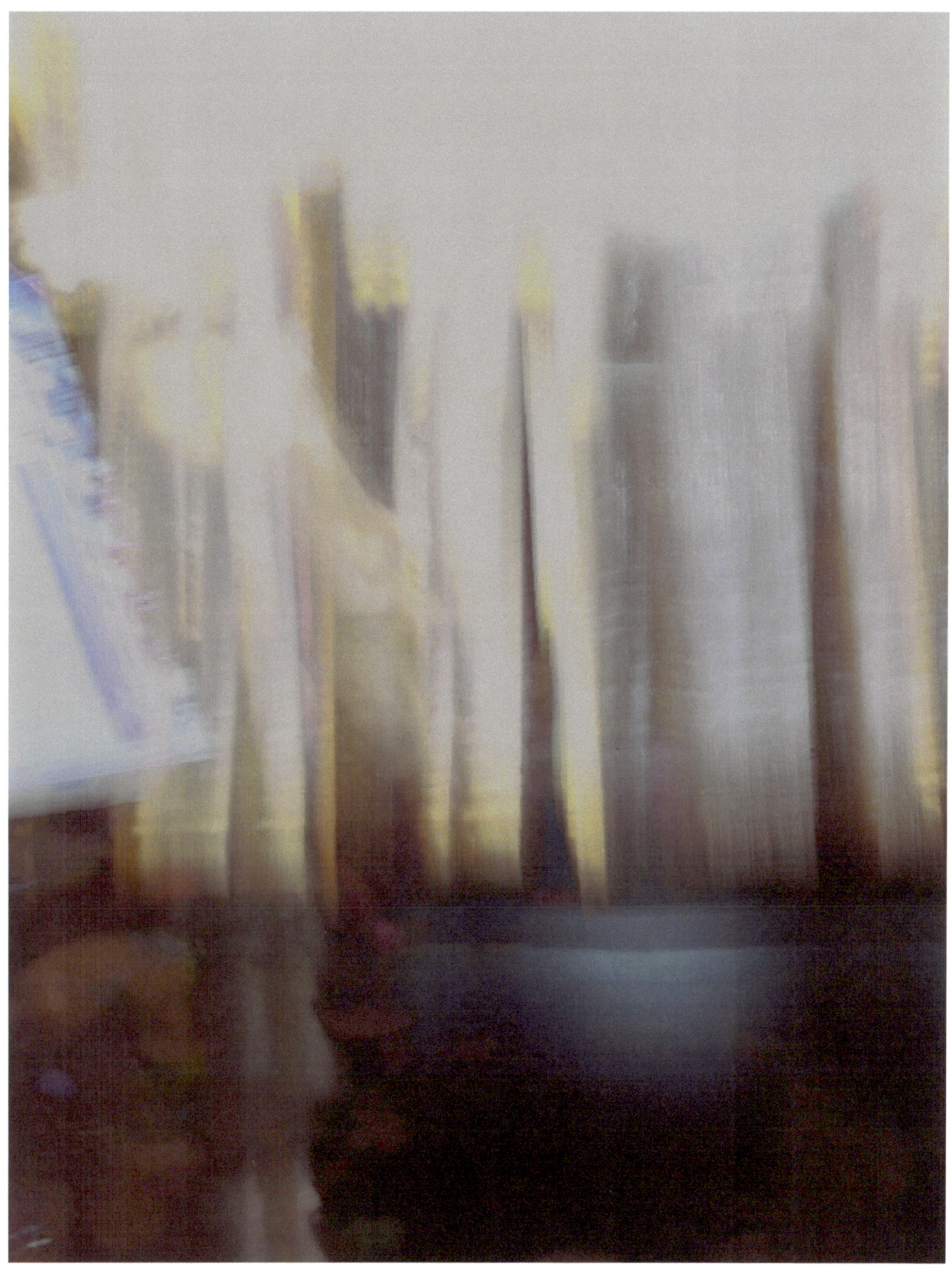

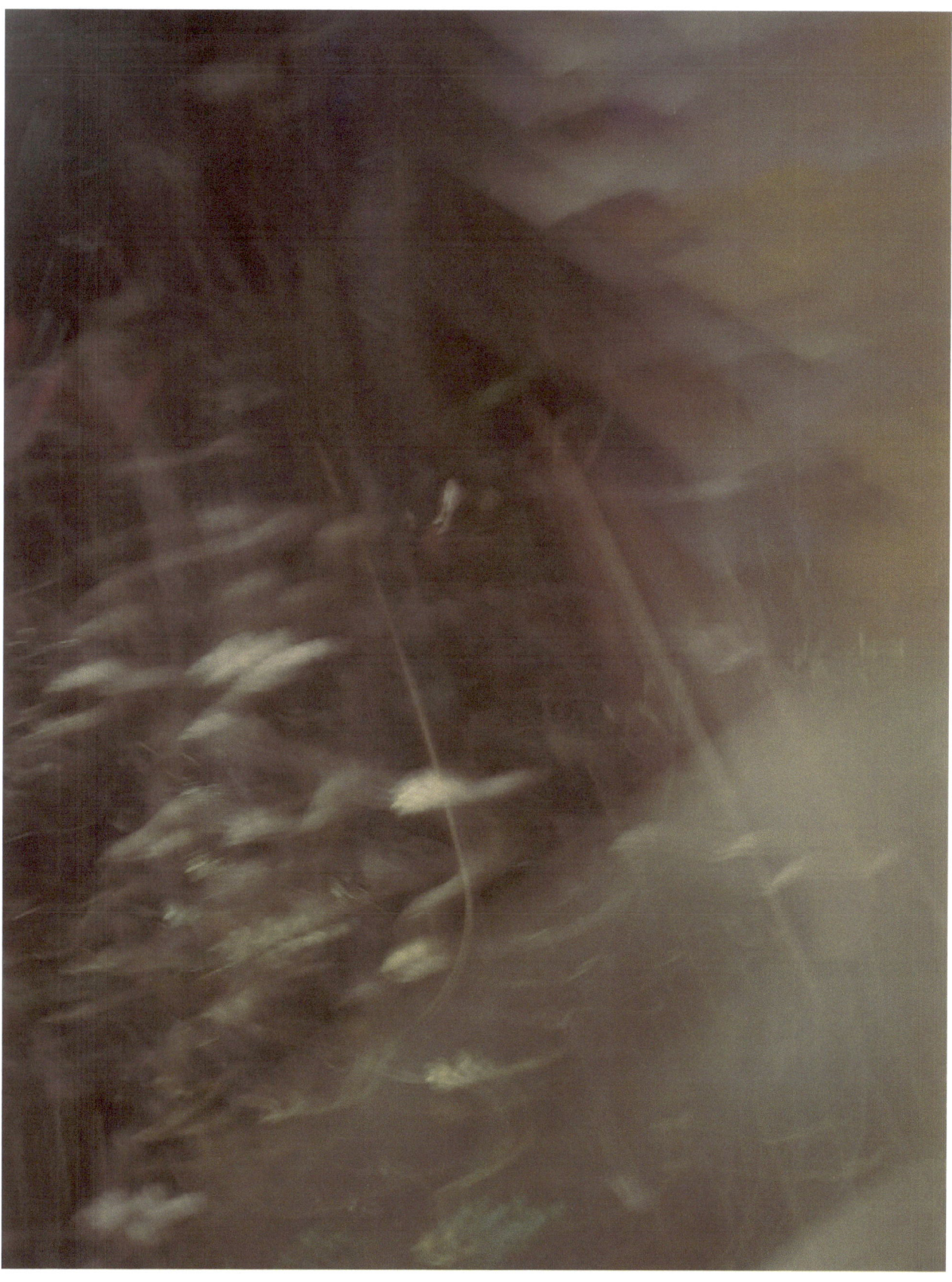

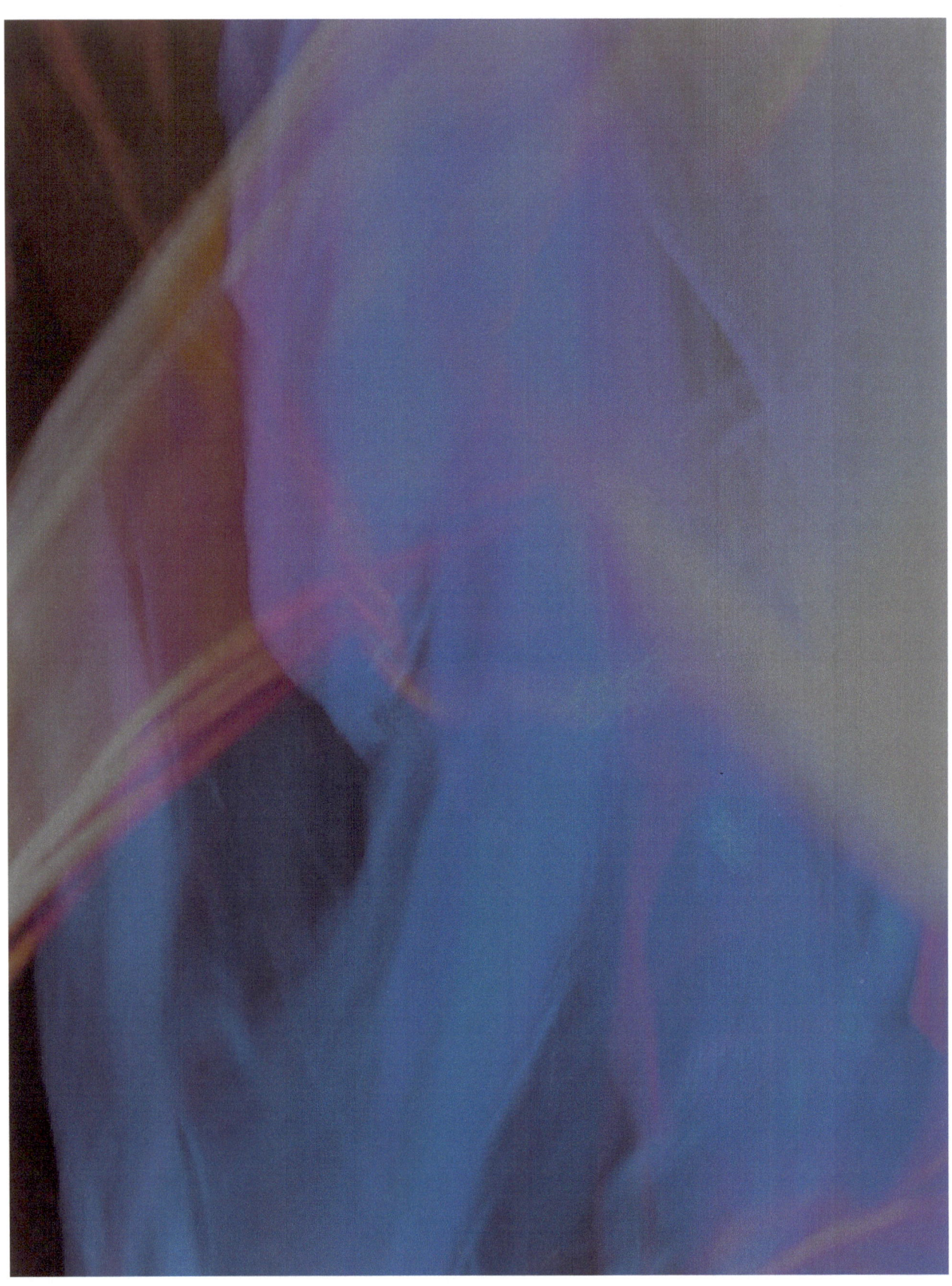

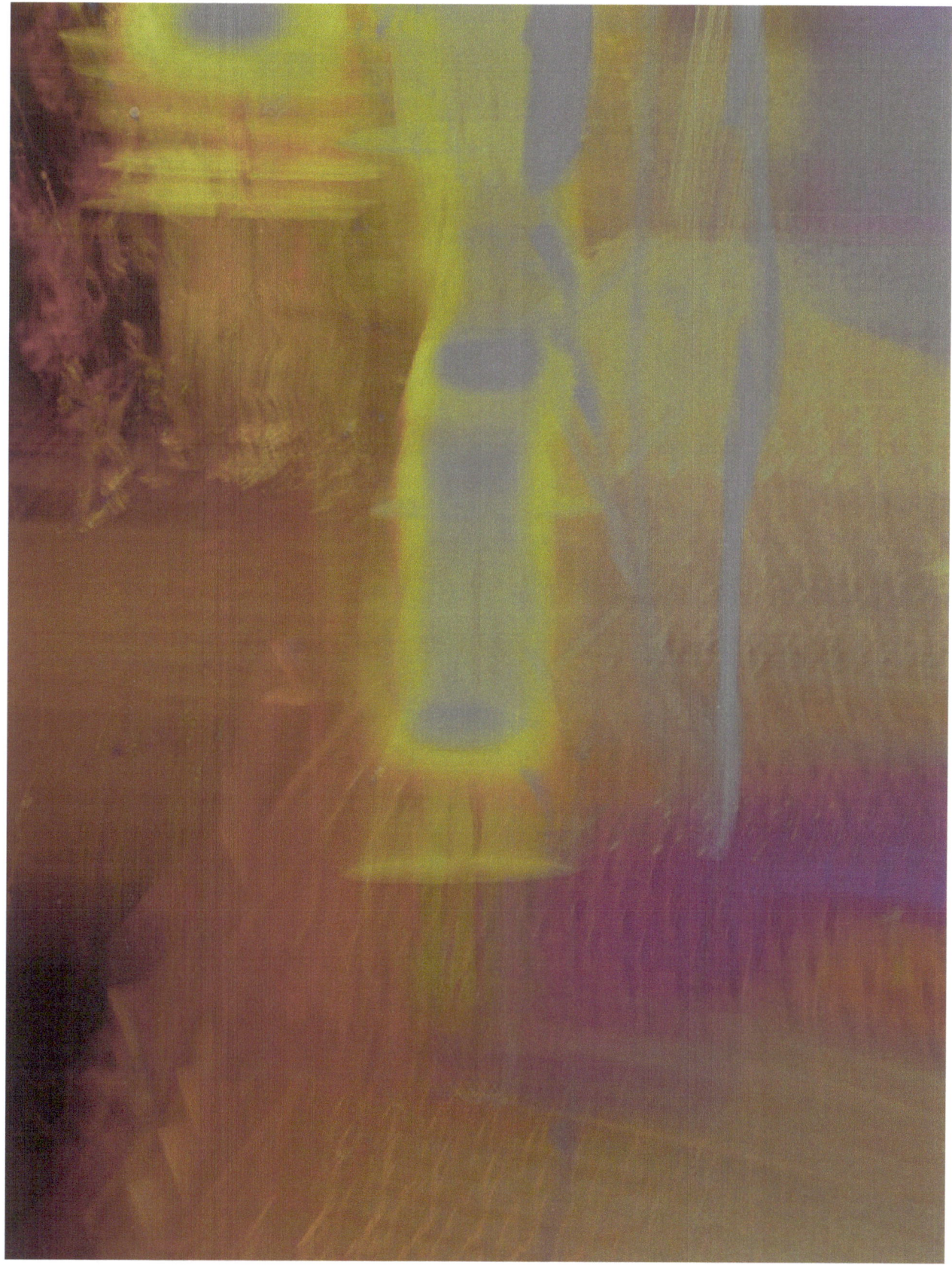

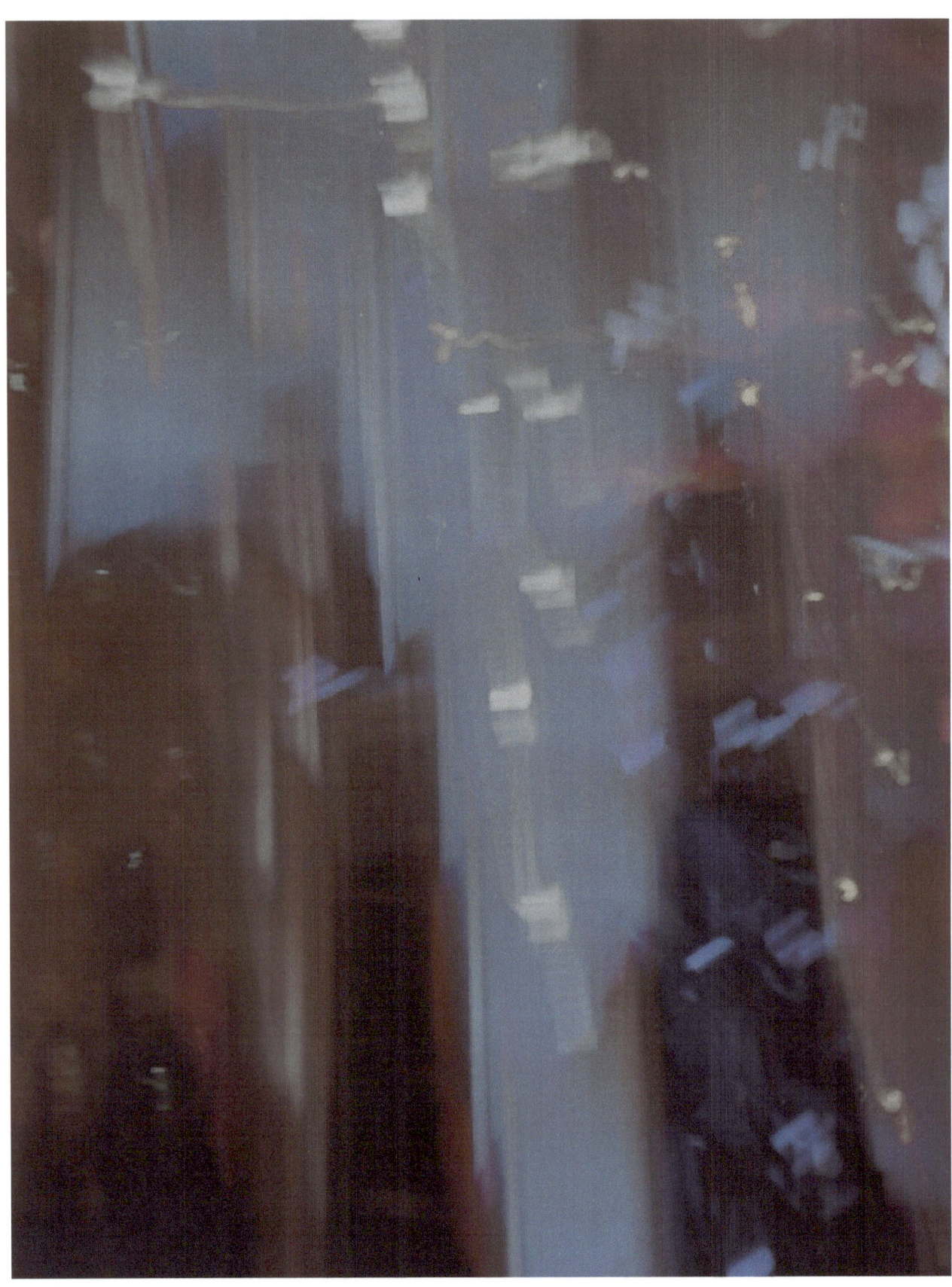

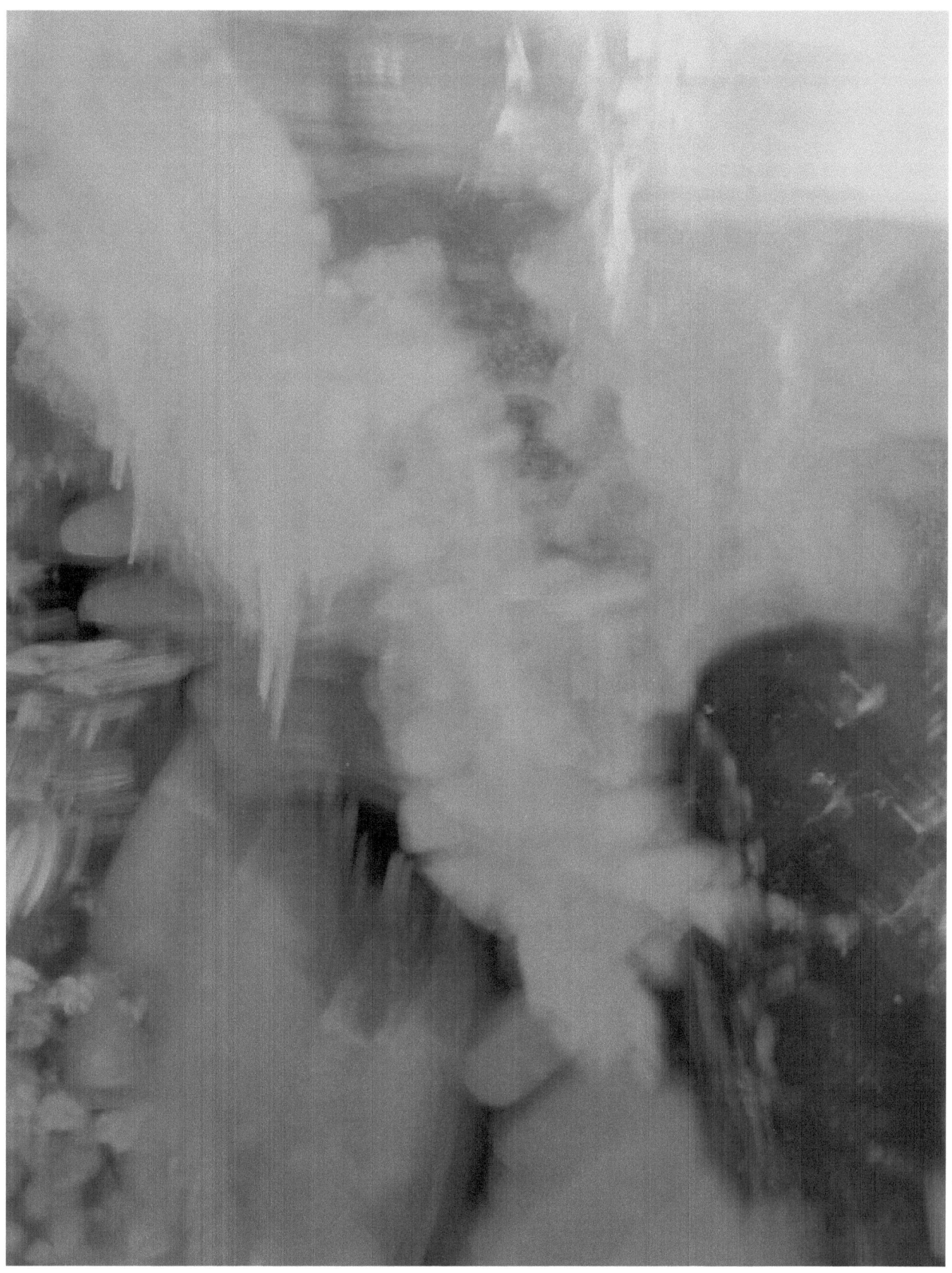

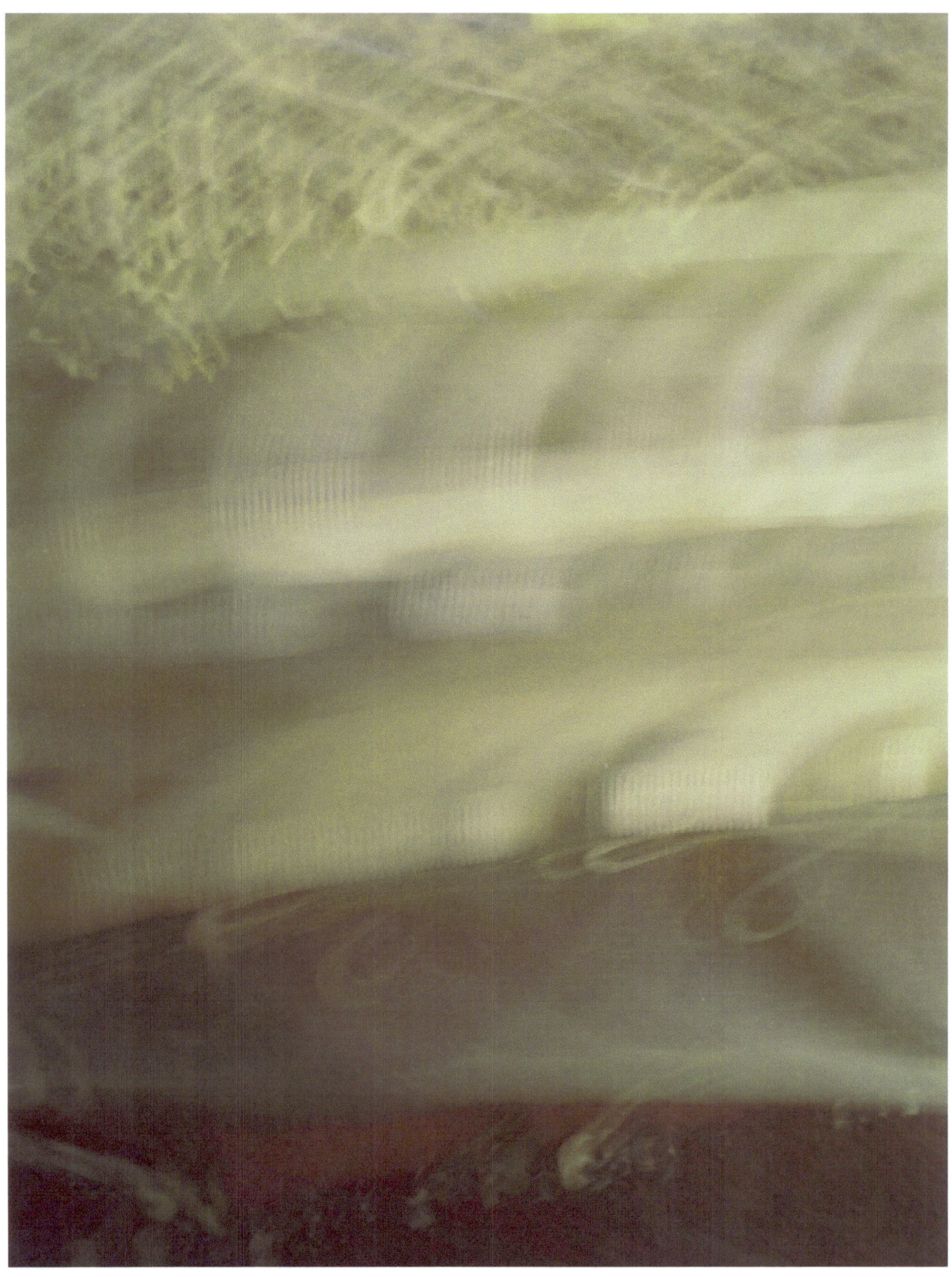

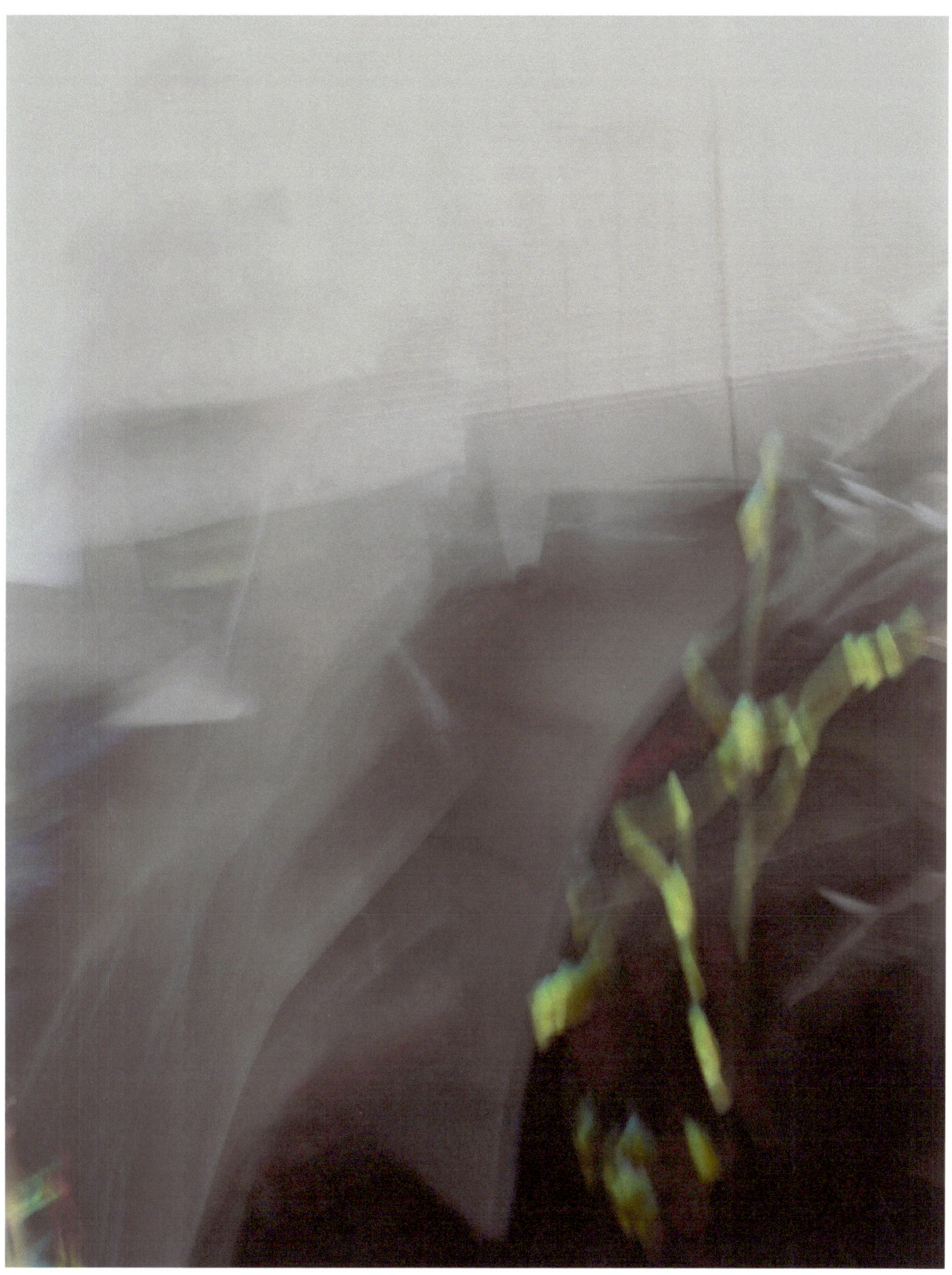

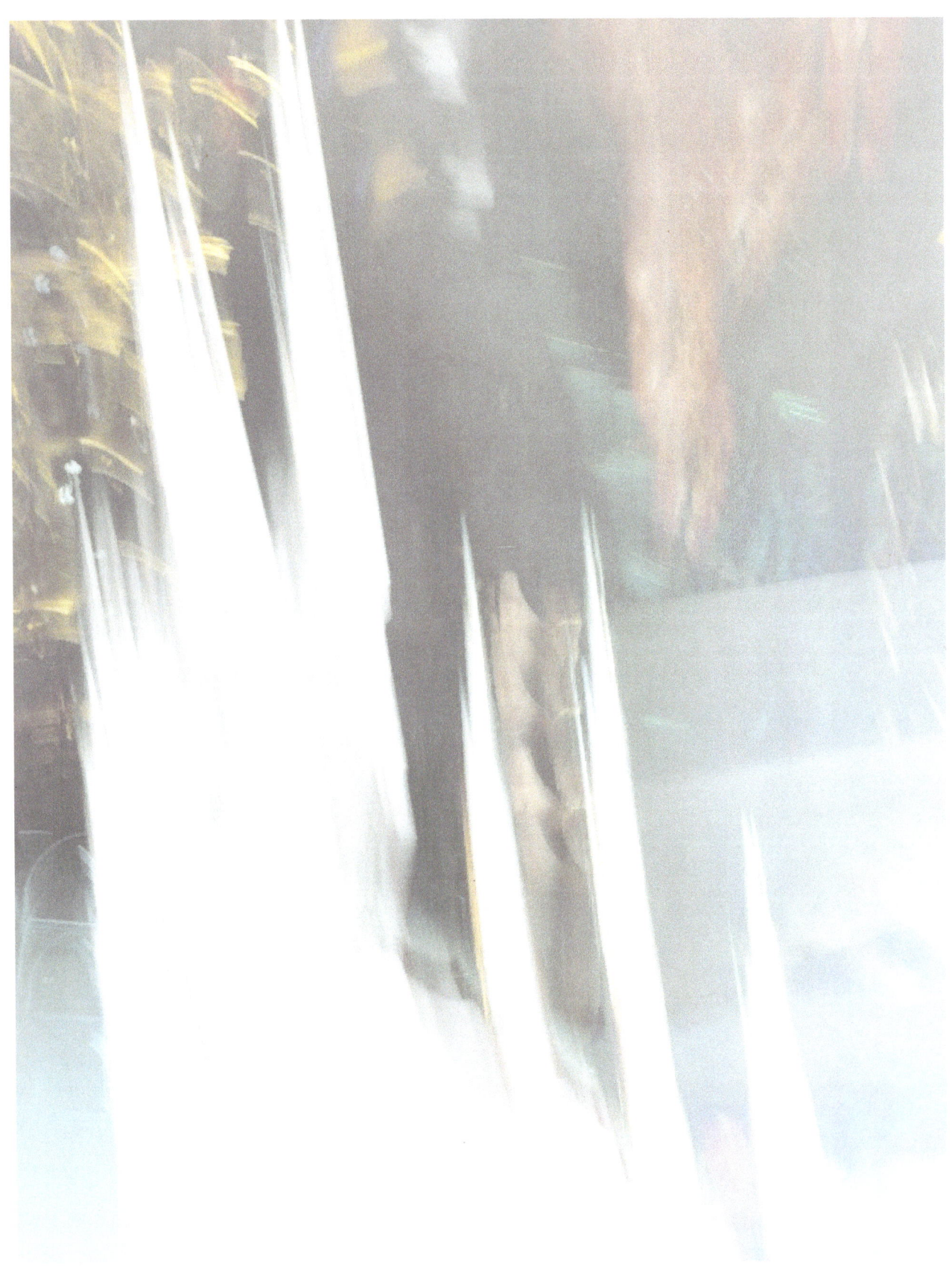

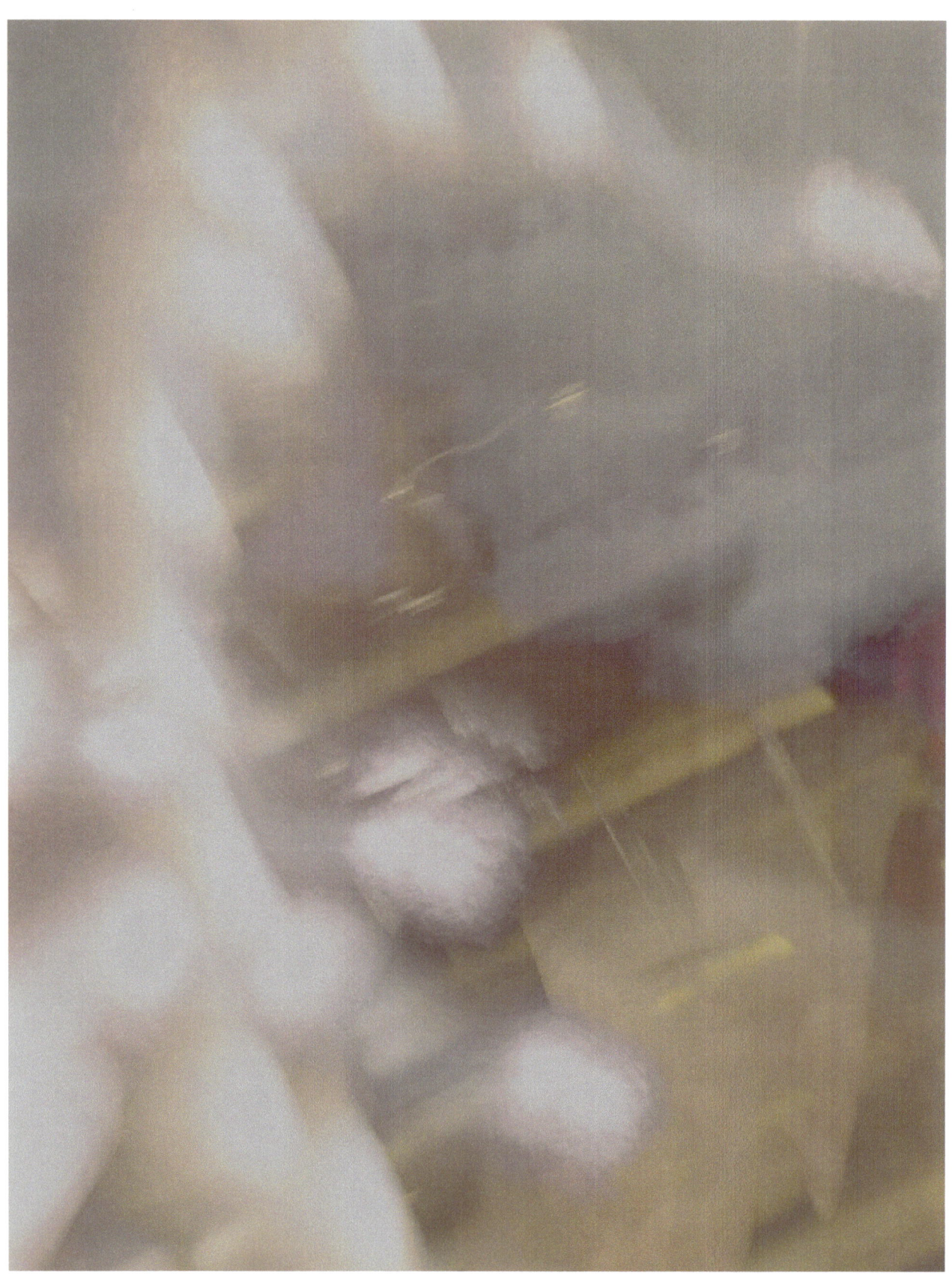

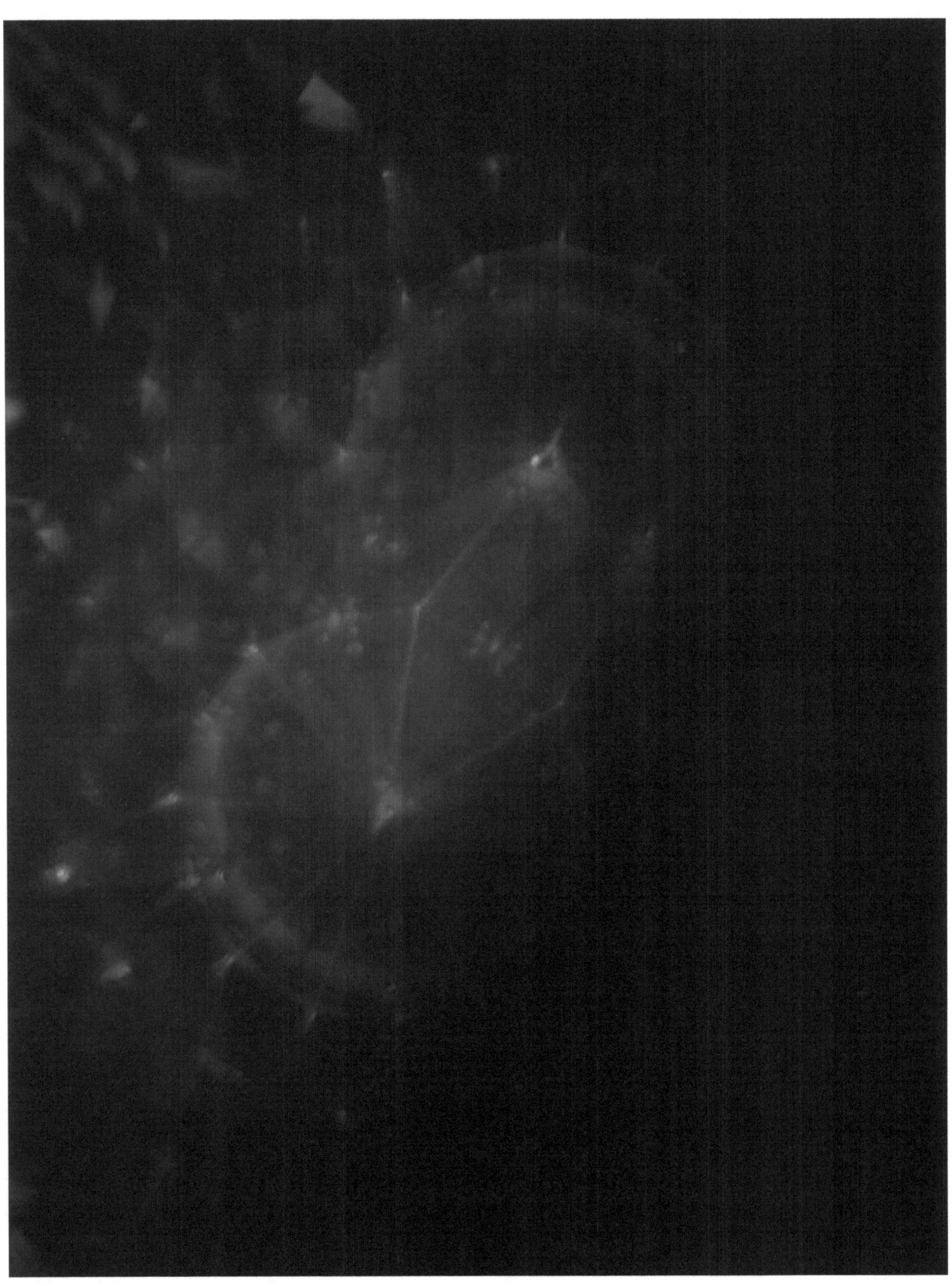

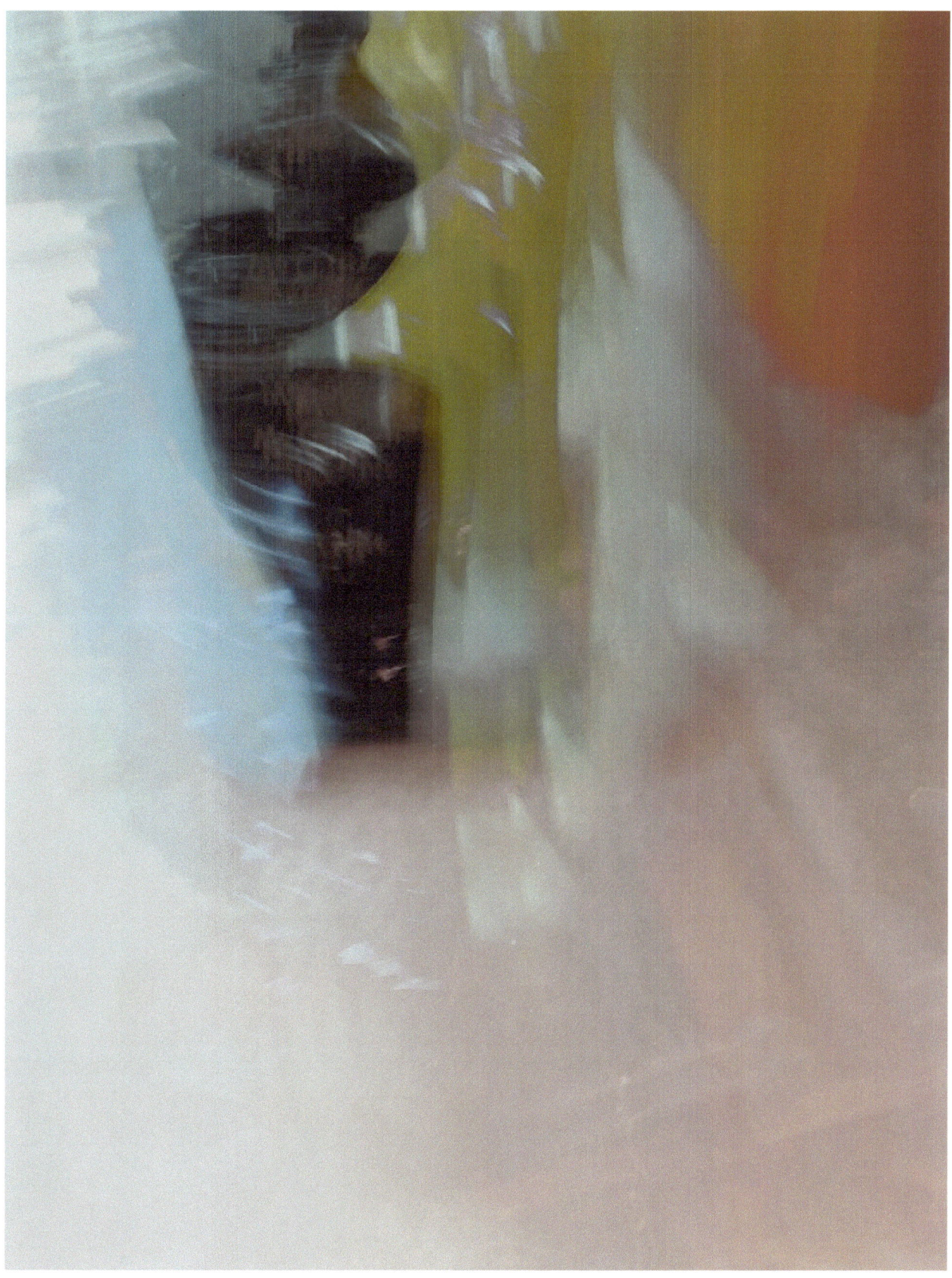

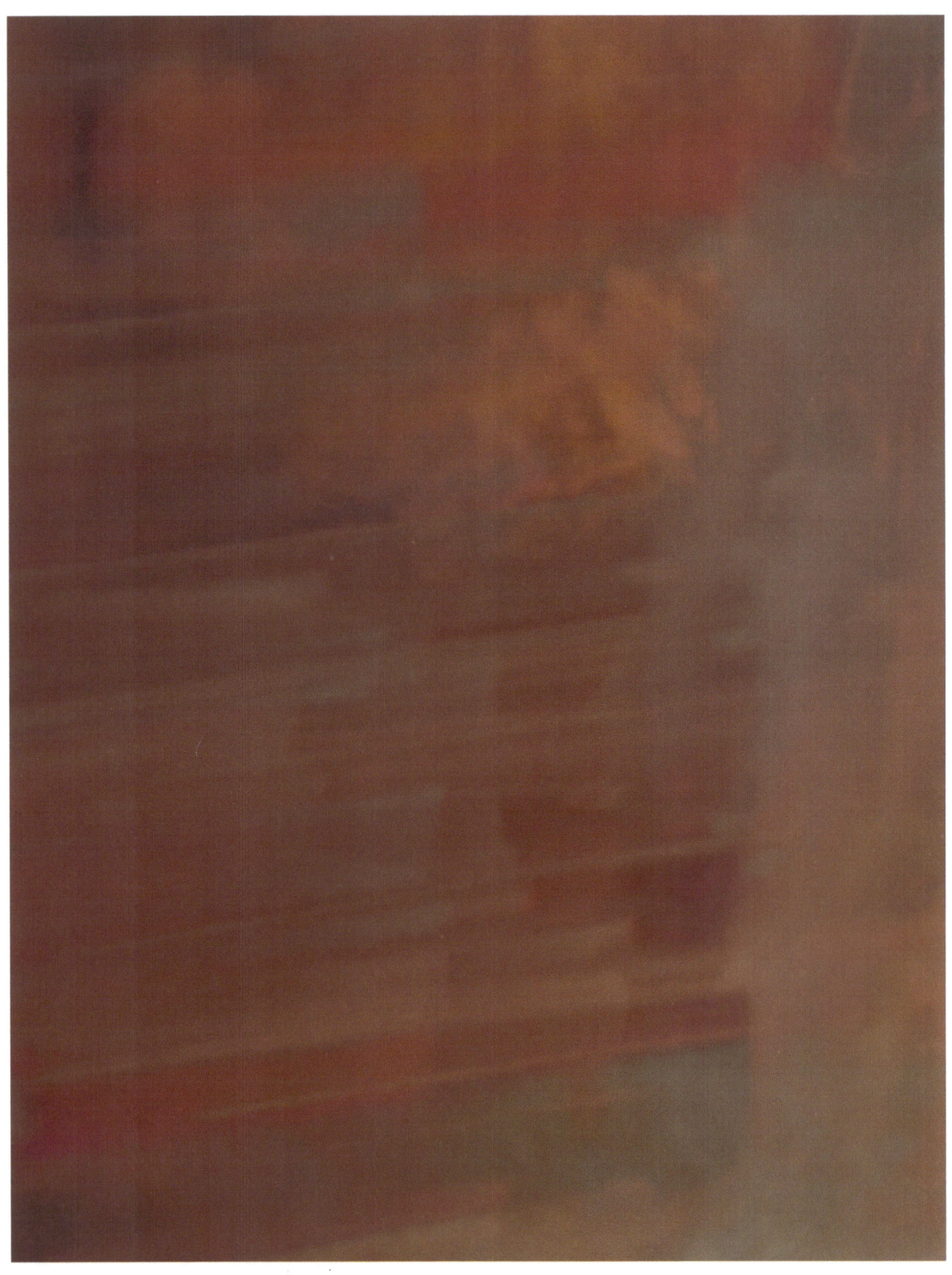

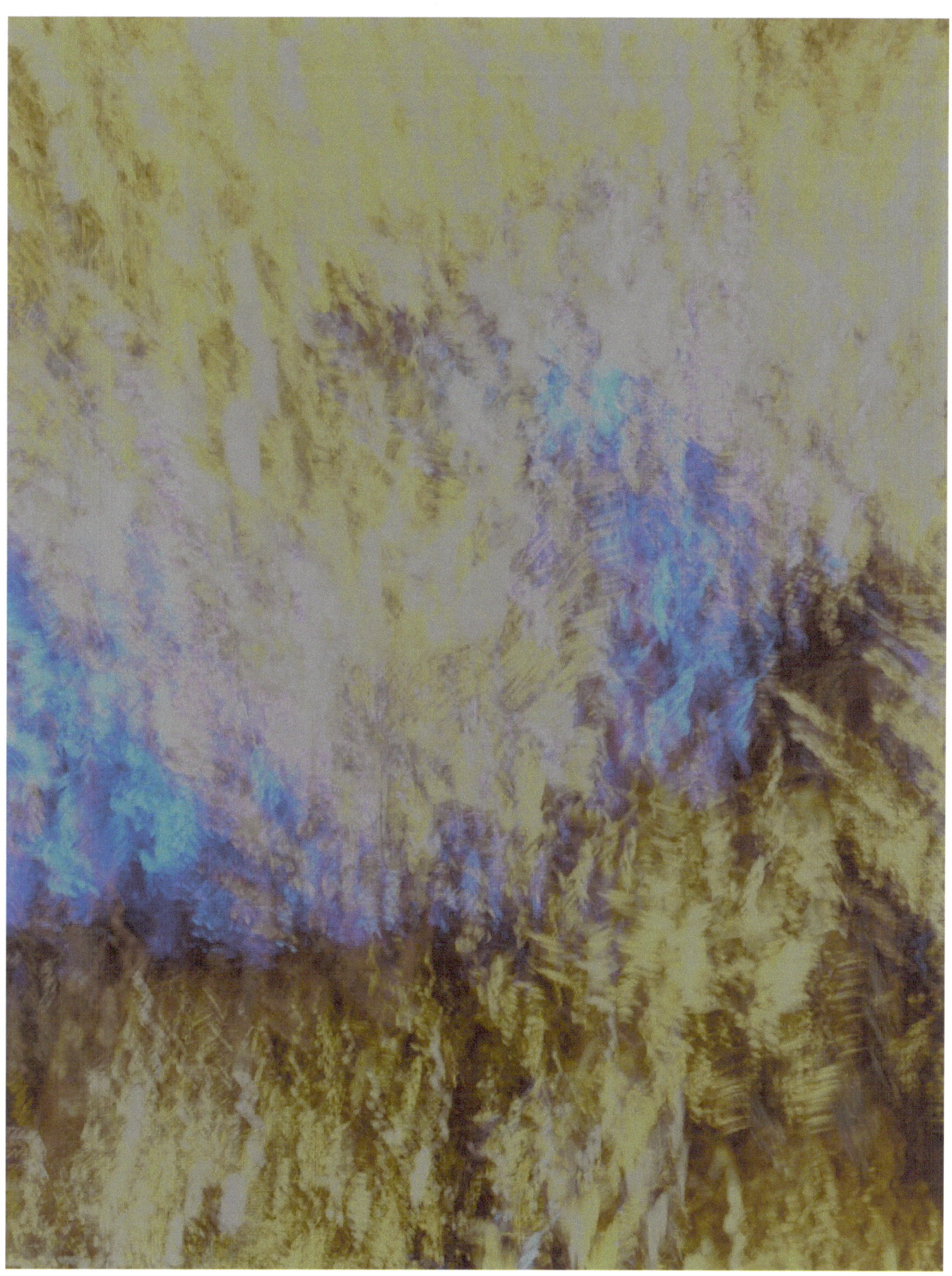

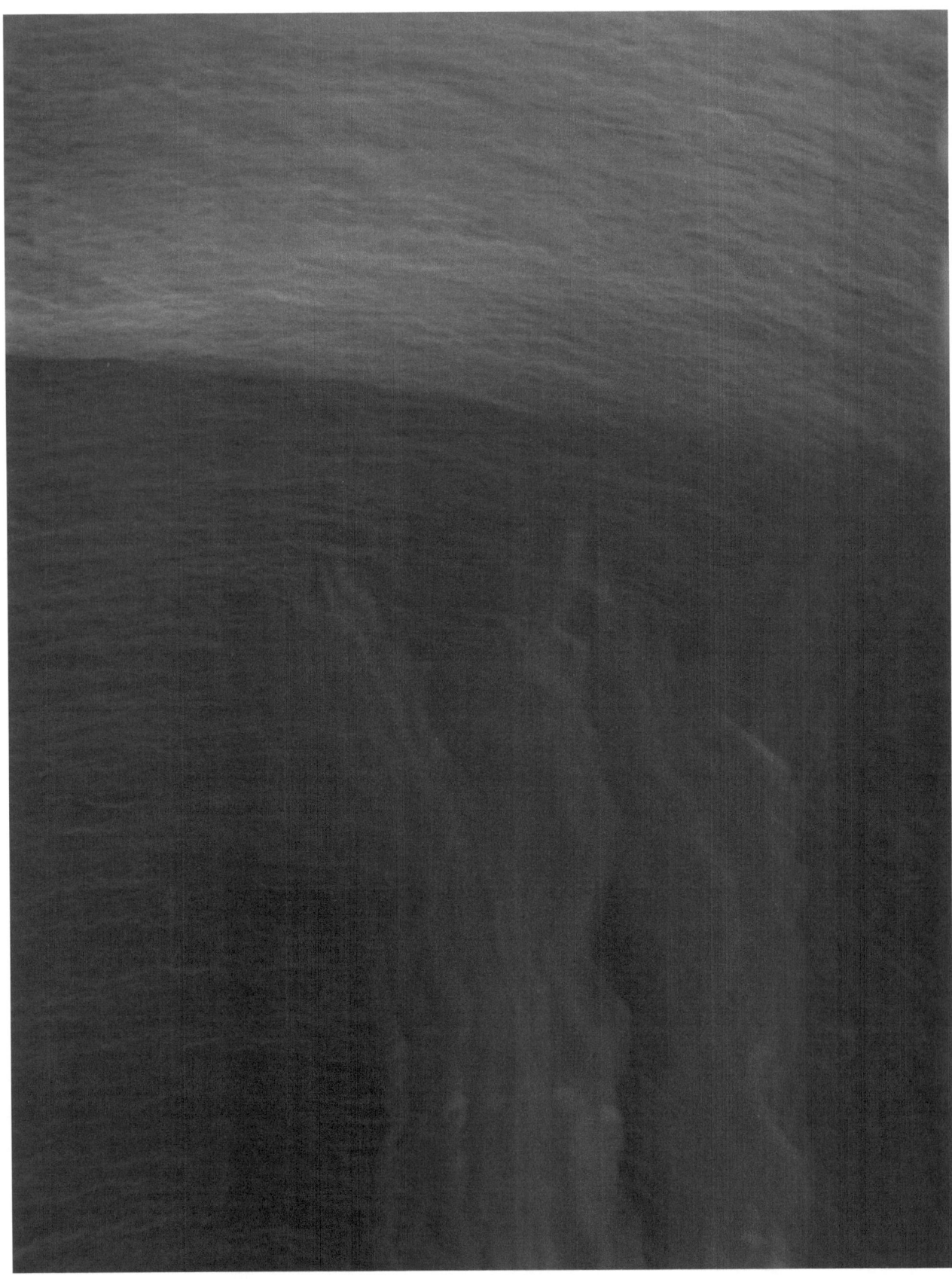